W9-BVB-591

DISCARD

Expressive Singing

Song Anthology

CALVIN COOLIDGE

LIBRARY

Volume Two
High Voice

Second Edition

Expressive Singing

Song Anthology

Selected, arranged, and edited by

Van A. Christy

Professor of Music, Emeritus

University of California
Santa Barbara

wcb
WM. C. BROWN COMPANY PUBLISHERS
DUBUQUE, IOWA 52001

SC
743.32
C468e
v.2

Publications by the Author

Wm. C. Brown Company Publishers

Expressive Singing Series:

> **Expressive Singing Textbook, Volume I**
>> Guidance, technical principles, exercises, and basics of interpretation

> **Expressive Singing Textbook, Volume II**
>> Pedagogy, production theory and technic, style and interpretation, song repertoire, principles of piano accompaniment, solo voice and piano accompaniment recordings

> **Expressive Singing Song Anthology, Volume I**
>> Songs in high, medium, and low voice editions designed primarily for the beginning student

> **Expressive Singing Song Anthology, Volume II**
>> Songs in high, medium, and low voice editions designed primarily for intermediate and advanced students

Foundations in Singing
> A basic textbook in guidance, exercises, and the fundamentals of technic and interpretation, including supplementary songs in medium-low and medium-high voice editions

Belwin-Mills Publishing Corp.

Fifty-seven Classic Period Songs (with Carl Zytowski)
> An anthology of select songs of Haydn, Mozart, Beethoven, and lesser known Classic Period composers, in medium-low and medium-high voice editions

Music Series

Consulting Editor
Frederick W. Westphal, Ph.D.
California State University, Sacramento

Copyright © 1961, 1966, 1983 by Wm. C. Brown Company Publishers

Library of Congress Catalog Card Number: 81-68955

ISBN 0-697-03532-8

All rights reserved. No part of this publication may be reproduced, stored in a retrieval system, or transmitted, in any form or by any means, electronic, mechanical, photocopying, recording, or otherwise, without the prior written permission of the publisher.

Printed in the United States of America

Contents by Song Type

Old English and Nineteenth-Century English

✱✱Old Italian

German Lieder

Modern French Impressionistic

✱Optional duet or solo

✱✱Original Italian text provided

Oratorio and Sacred

Opera

Appendixes

✳ Optional duet or solo
✳✳ Original Italian text provided

Contents by Song Title

*Optional solo or duet

Preface to the Second Edition

These song anthologies, *Volume I* and *Volume II*, were designed to provide a varied and balanced collection of songs from the standard repertoire that in the experience of many voice teachers not only accomplish the objectives of developing a sound vocal technic but are suitable for and attractive to college-level students. The cooperation and advice of a number of outstanding college and university voice teachers, who were consulted to establish the most useful song collection, are gratefully acknowledged.

The needs of all voice ranges are accommodated by publishing the anthologies in three editions: *Low, Medium,* and *High.* The *Medium Voice Edition* will be found the most practical for ensemble classwork and for the majority of beginning students. Individual students whose voices are quite low or high should select, after consultation with their instructor, the edition that best suits their voice needs at the time.

Songs in these anthologies were selected with four major objectives in mind: (1) the vocal needs and interests of beginning students were considered of prime importance; (2) only songs of artistic worth that would be of interest for concert programming were included; (3) the total content was chosen to include a variety of favorite song literature that experienced teachers have found of greatest value in developing singing technic, and (4) the attractiveness of the songs to both student and teacher was an important factor.

Although all songs, except the new ballad and folk song settings by the author, are from standard recital repertoire, they are within the capability of most students to perform effectively. In *Song Anthology, Volume I,* vocal range is limited to an octave and a third in most instances; and in *Song Anthology, Volume II,* the range is limited to an octave and a fourth. The range is indicated on the title page of each song. In addition, sustained tessitura was given careful consideration before choosing the proper key for the songs in each of the three voice editions.

Eleven new songs have been added to the second edition of *Volume I.* An unusually wide variety of styles and moods is represented in the collection, which includes art songs, Old Italian songs, sacred songs, spirituals, ballads, and folk songs of a beginning or lower intermediate level of difficulty.

Volume II has thirteen new songs. Styles represented include Old English, Old Italian, German lieder, French Impressionistic, oratorio, and opera. A major thrust of this second edition was to strengthen the first three groups. Most songs in *Volume II* are of an intermediate level of difficulty, with a few included of a greater challenge.

There are seven optional duets in *Volume I* and four in *Volume II,* which students often find stimulating and challenging. All songs are edited carefully in detail in regard to dynamics, tempo, and phrasing. Recommended length of phrases is marked with an apostrophe and, where needed, optional places for breathing are indicated with an encircled apostrophe.

Song Anthology, Volume I, features songs in English. However, the original texts of art songs in non-English languages and their English texts are also provided.

Song Anthology, Volume II, with the exception of songs originally in English, features songs in languages other than English, with an English translation provided. Rules for Italian, German, and French pronunciation will be found in the Appendixes of each volume.

In order to provide maximum assistance to the student, specific suggestions in respect to style, mood, generally prevailing tone color, and specific suggestions on interpretation of each song will also be found in the Appendixes. These should be read carefully before starting a song. Suggestions provided here and interpretive markings in the scores should be followed unless the teacher has other preferences. For the convenience of the user, this new edition presents all two-page songs in open book arrangement, so that page turning is unnecessary.

There is a careful correlation between the *Expressive Singing, Volume I Textbook,* and the *Expressive Singing Song Anthology, Volume I* and *Volume II.* Together they form a complete course of study, although the text and the anthologies may also be used independently. Beginning vocal students will find *Song Anthology, Volume I,* ideal for accompanying the theory of vocal production and vocal exercises in the first part of the *Expressive Singing, Volume I Textbook.* Intermediate and advanced students will find *Song Anthology, Volume II,* equally suitable for integration with the latter chapters of theory and exercises of the textbook. *Expressive Singing, Volume II Textbook,* primarily pedagogy and extensive information for the teacher, is correlated carefully with *Volume I Textbook,* primarily for the student.

Expressive Singing

Song Anthology

LOVE HAS EYES

Charles Dibdin

Sir Henry Bishop

Edited by Van A. Christy

1. Love's blind they say,___ Oh, nev-er nay,___ Can words love's
2. Love's wing'd they cry,___ Oh, nev-er I___ No pin - ions

grace__im-part,___ The fan-cy weak,___ The tongue may speak,___
have__to__soar,___ De-ceiv-ers rove,___ But nev-er love,___

But eyes__a-lone the heart, In one soft
At-tach'd,__he__roves no more! Can he have

look what lan-guage lies, Oh, yes, be-lieve me, Love has
wings who nev-er flies? And yes, be-lieve me, Love has

eyes, Oh,___ love has ___ eyes, _____ 'Love has eyes,_Oh,__
eyes, Oh,___ love has ___ eyes, _____

*Optional second time only

4

love has eyes, ____ Oh, yes, be-lieve___me, ____ love has eyes,

Oh, ___ yes, be-lieve ___ me, Oh, ___ yes, be-lieve me, Oh, ___ yes, be-lieve ___ me, ___

love has _____ eyes. _____

*High notes optional second time only; trill optional, but sing the *portamento* anticipation.

HAVE YOU SEEN BUT A
WHITE LILLIE GROW

Ben Jonson

Composer unknown

Edited by Van A. Christy

Or swan's down ev - er, Or have smelt of the bud of the bri - er,*

Or the nard in the fire, Or have tast - ed the bag of the bee; Oh, so

white, Oh, so soft, Oh, so sweet, so sweet, so sweet is she! Oh, so

white, Oh, so soft, Oh, so sweet, so sweet,___ so sweet is she!

*optional to sing as a half-note single-syllable word.

BLOW, BLOW, THOU WINTER WIND

From *As You Like It* by
William Shakespeare

Thomas Augustine Arne

Edited by Van A. Christy

Thy tooth is not so keen, _____ be - cause thou art not ___ seen, ___ thy ___
Tho' thou the wa-ters warp, _____ Thy sting is ___ not ___ so ___ sharp ___ thy ___

tooth ___ is ___ not so ___ keen, _____ be - cause thou art not seen, ___ al -
sting ___ is ___ not ___ so ___ sharp, _____ as friend re - mem-ber'd not. ___ Thy

cresc.

tho' ___ thy ___ breath be rude, al - tho' ___ thy ___ breath be rude, _____ al -
sting ___ is ___ not so sharp, as friend re - mem - ber'd not, _____ as ___

poco a poco cresc.

D.S. second verse

tho' ___ thy ___ breath ___ be ___ rude.
friend re - mem - ber' not.

D.S. second verse

*optional second time only.

9

THE LASS WITH THE DELICATE AIR

Thomas Augustine Arne

Edited by Van A. Christy

1. Young Mol - ly who___ lived at the foot___ of___ the___ hill, Whose
2. One eve-ning last___ May, as I trav-ersed the___ grove, In

fame___ ev' - ry___ maid - en with en - vy doth fill, Of
thought - less re - tire - ment, not dream - ing of love, I

beau - ty___ is ___ bless'd with ___ so ___ am - ple a
chanced to___ es - py the ___ gay ___ nymph, I ___ de -

share,____ Men call her__the____ lass with the del - i - cate
clare,____ And real-ly__she____ had a most del - i - cate

air, with the del - - - - - - - - i-cate
air, a most del - - - - - - - - i-cate

air,____ Men call__her__the__lass__with__the__del - i - cate
air,____ And real - ly__she__had__a__most__del - i - cate

air. 3. By a mur-mur-ing____ brook, on a
air. 4. A____ thou-sand times__o'er I've re -

11

green—moss-y — bed, A chap-let—com-pos-ing, the
peat-ed—my—suit, But still—the—tor-men-tor af-

fair—one was laid; Sur-prised and—trans-port-ed—I—
fects—to be mute! Then tell me—ye swains who—have—

could not—for-bear—With—rap-ture—to—gaze on her
con-quered—the—fair,—How to win the—dear lass with the

del - i - cate air, on her del - - -
del - i - cate air, with the del - - -

12

*Small notes optional for high voices

13

A PASTORAL

Henry Carey

Henry Carey

Edited and Arranged by Van A. Christy

*Trill optional

IT WAS A LOVER AND HIS LASS

William Shakespeare

Thomas Morley

Edited and arranged by
Granville Bantock and Van A. Christy

1. It was a lov - er and his lass,
2. Be - tween the a - cres of the rye, } With a
3. This car - ol they be - gan that hour,
4. Then, pret - ty lov - ers take the time,

hey, with a ho, with a hey, non-ne-no, And a hey, non-ne-no, ne-

no,

That o'er the green corn - field did pass,
These pret - ty coun - try fools did lie }
How that life was but a flow'r } In
For love is crown - ed with the prime,

spring - time, in spring - time, in spring - time, The on - ly pret - ty

ring - time, When birds do sing, Hey ding a ding a ding, Hey ding a ding a ding, Hey

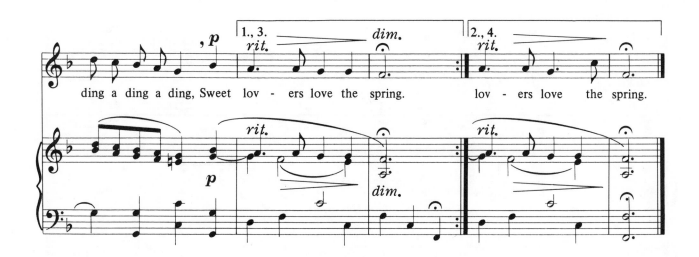

ding a ding a ding, Sweet lov - ers love the spring. lov - ers love the spring.

COME UNTO THESE YELLOW SANDS

From *The Tempest*
by William Shakespeare

Henry Purcell

*Edited and Arranged by Van A. Christy

*Optional solo or duet

18

I ATTEMPT FROM LOVE'S SICKNESS TO FLY

Henry Purcell

Edited by Van A. Christy

fe - ver, Since I am my - self, my own fe - ver — and — pain. No

more now, no more now, fond — heart, with pride should we swell, Thou

canst not — raise — forc - es, thou canst not — raise — forc - es e - nough to re-

bel, I at - tempt from Love's sick - ness to fly _____ in _____

make us seek ru - in, and love those that hate. I at-tempt from Love's

sick-ness to fly_____ in__ vain,__ Since I am my-

self, my own fe - ver, Since I am my - self, my own fe - ver and__

pain.__

*Trill optional

NOW SLEEPS THE CRIMSON PETAL

Alfred Lord Tennyson

Roger Quilter

MY LOVELY CELIA

George Monro

George Monro

Edited and Arranged by Van A. Christy

love - ly___ Ce - lia, heav'n - ly___ fair, As

li - lies___ sweet, as soft___ as___

air, No more,___ then, tor - ment__me,

but _____ be _____ kind, And with _____ your _____

love__ ease my trou - bled mind.

Oh, let _____ me _____

27

gaze _____ on your _____ bright _ eyes, Where melt - ing _____

beams so oft _____ a - rise, My heart's _____ en -

chant-ed with _____ thy _ charms, Oh, take _____ me,

dy - ing, to _____ your arms. _____

28

WEEP YOU NO MORE, SAD FOUNTAINS

Author unknown

Roger Quilter

Edited by Van A. Christy

Poco andante ♩=56

mp

Weep you no more, sad foun - tains; What need you flow so fast? Look how the snow-y moun - tains Heav'n's sun doth gent - ly waste! But my Sun's heav'n-ly

eyes View not your weep - ing, That now lies sleep - ing,

Soft - ly now soft - ly lies Sleep - ing, sleep -

ing. Sleep is a re - con - cil - ing, A

rest that peace be - gets; Doth not the sun rise

smil - ing When fair at even he sets? _____ Rest you, then, rest, sad

eyes! Melt not in weep - ing, While she lies sleep - ing,

Soft - ly now soft - ly lies Sleep - ing, sleep - -

ing.

ORPHEUS WITH HIS LUTE

From *Henry VIII* by
William Shakespeare

Sir Arthur Sullivan

Edited by Van A. Christy

selves, when he ___ did sing. Or -

- - - pheus with his lute, with his lute made___

trees, And the moun - tain tops that freeze Bow them -

selves when he ___ did sing, Bow ___ them -

selves when he _____ did sing.

To his mu - sic _____ plants and flow'rs e - ver

sprung: as sun and show'rs There had made a last-ing

spring, To his mu - sic plants _____ and flow'rs e - ver

sprung: _____ as sun and show-ers There had made a last - - - ing spring.

Ev' - - - -

35

*Trill optional

In sweet mu - sic is _____ such art,

Kill - ing care and grief of __ heart,

In sweet mu - sic is _____ such

art, _____ Kill - ing __ care _____ and __

*Optional for high voice mezza voce

VICTORIOUS, MY HEART IS!

(Vittoria, mio core!)

Giacomo Carissimi

English text by H. Millard

Edited by Van A. Christy

Allegro con brio (♩ =168)

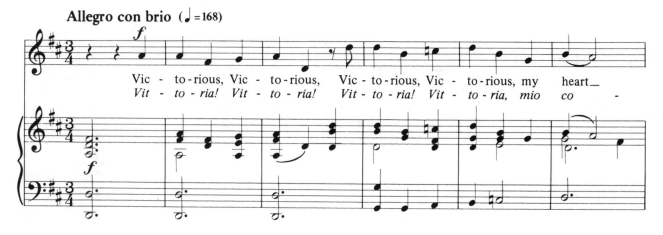

Vic - to - rious, Vic - to - rious, Vic - to - rious, Vic - to - rious, my heart
Vit - to - ria! Vit - to - ria! Vit - to - ria! Vit - to - ria, mio co -

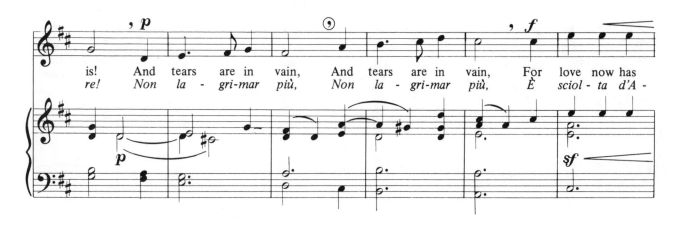

is! And tears are in vain, And tears are in vain, For love now has
re! Non la - gri - mar più, Non la - gri - mar più, È sciol - ta d'A -

bro - ken its bonds_ in twain; Vic - to - rious, Vic - to - rious, my heart_ is! And
mo - re La vil ser - vi - tù; Vit - to - ria! Vit - to - ria, mio co - re! Non

tears are in vain, For love now has bro-ken its bonds in twain, For
la - gri-mar più, È sciol-ta d'A - mo-re La vil ser - vi-tù, È

love
sciol - - - - - - - - - now has bro-ken its
ta d'A - mo-re La

bonds in twain. The false one is van-quish'd, her glan-ces a-muse me, De-
ser - vi-tù. Già l'em-pia a' tuoi dan - ni, Fra stuo-lo di sguar-di, Con

cep-tion no long-er with arts can con-fuse me! No false-hood or
vez - zi bu - giar-di Di - spo-se gl'in - gan - ni; Le fro - de, gli af-

now has bro-ken its bonds __ in twain!
ta d'A - mo - re La - ser - vi - tù!

meno mosso e dolce assai

Her smile once en-tran-cing no darts is re-veal-ing, The wounds in my
Da lu - ci ri - den - ti Non e-sce più stra - le, Che pia-ga mor-

p meno mosso e dolce assai

bo-som with time are_ all_ heal - ing; All sor-row and tor-ment no
ta - le Nel pet - to_ m'av - ven - ti: Nel duol, ne' tor - men - ti lo

cresc.

long - er I'm fear - ing, Now bro-ken each tie is, all fears dis-ap-
più non mi sfac - cio È rot-to o-gni lac-cio, Spa - ri - to il ti-

FAIREST ADORED
(Alma del core)

Antonio Caldara

English text by Everett Helm

Edited by Van A. Christy

Tempo di menuetto

Fair-est a - dor - ed, Spir-it_ of_ beau-ty!
Al - ma del co - re, spir-to_ dell' al - ma!

Fair-est a - dor - ed, Spir-it of_ beau-ty! Thy faith-ful lov - er__ I'll ev - er
Al - ma del co - re, spir-to_ dell' al - ma, sem-pre co - stan - te__ t'a - do - re-

*optional

*optional

ev— er be, I'll ev— er— be, I'll _____ ev— er be.
_do — re — rò,_ _t'a-do-re-rò, t'a — do-re-rò!_

Fair— est a— dor— ed, Spir— it of_ beau-ty, Thy faith-ful lov— er_____
Al — ma del co — re, spir-to _dell'_ _al — ma,_ _sem-pre co- stan — te_____

I'll_ ev— er_ be, Thy faith-ful lov— er I'll ev— er be.
_t'a-do — re-rò, sem-pre co - stan-te____ t'a-do-re-rò._

*optional

47

WHEN ON THE SURGING WAVE
(Come raggio di sol)

Antonio Caldara

English text by Van A. Christy

Edited by Van A. Christy

VIRGIN, FOUNT OF LOVE
(Vergin, tutto amor)

Francesco Durante

*Edited by Van A. Christy
from the Alessandro Parisotti setting

English text by Theodore Baker

Vir - gin, fount of love, Dear Moth - er, thou of
Ver - gin, tut - to a - mor, o ma - dre di bon -

*Used by permission of G. Schirmer, Inc., holders of the original copyright.

mer-cy, whose heart was riv-en, whose heart was riv - en, O heark - en, Queen____ of
ta — de, o ma-dre pi — a, ma-dre pi — a, a-scol — ta, dol - ce Ma —

Heav-en, Hearken to a sin - ner's cry,___ to a sin - ner's cry.
ri — a, la_____ vo-ce del pec-ca-tor,___del___ pec - ca - tor.

Let kind com-pas-sion move thee In mer-cy hear her sad la -
Il pian - to suo ti muo-va, guingano a te i suoi la -

ment - ing, Her mourn-ful moan as-cend-ing Un-to thy throne of grace___on
men - ti, suo duol, suoi tri-sti ac - cen - ti, sen-ti pie-to - so quel___tuo

DEAR LOVE OF MINE
(Caro mio ben)

Giuseppe Giordani

English text by Van A. Christy

Edited and Arranged by Van A. Christy

IF THOU LOV'ST ME

(Se tu m'ami)

Giovanni Battista Pergolesi

English text by Theodore Baker

If thou_ lov'st me,_ and sigh - est ev - er But_ for me,_ O gen - tle_
Se tu_ m'a - mi,_ se tu so - spi - ri Sol_ per me,_gen - til_ pa -

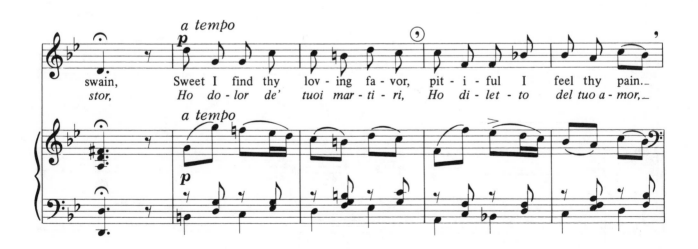

swain, Sweet I find thy lov - ing fa - vor, pit - i - ful I feel thy pain._
stor, Ho do - lor de' tuoi mar - ti - ri, Ho di - let - to del tuo a - mor,_

Should'st thou think tho', that de - mure-ly I on thee a - lone may smile,
Ma se pen - si che so - let - to Io ti deb - ba ri - a - mar,

Sim - ple shep-herd, thou art sure-ly Prone thy sen - ses to be-guile; Sim - ple shep-herd,
Pa - sto-rel - lo, sei sog-get - to Fa - cil-men-te a t'in - gan-nar; Pa - sto-rel - lo,

thou art sure-ly Prone thy sen - ses to be-guile, prone thy sen - ses to be-guile.
sei sog-get - to Fa - cil men-te a t'in-gan-nar, Fa - cil men-te a t'in-gan-nar.

As a fair red rose, a - lov - er Fain might Syl - via choose to - day, Hap-ly if he
Bel - la ro - sa por-po - ri - na Og - gi Sil-via sce - glie-rà, Con la scu - sa

59

me,— O gen - tle— swain, Sweet I find thy lov - ing fa - vor, Pit - i - ful I
me,—gen - til— pa - stor, *Ho do - lor de' tuoi mar - ti - ri,* *Ho di - let - to*

feel thy pain.— Should'st thou think tho' that de-mure-ly I on thee a - lone— may smile,
del tuo a - mor,— Ma se pen - si che so - let - to Io ti deb ba ri - a - mar,

Sim - ple shep-herd, thou art sure-ly Prone thy sen - ses to be-guile; Sim - ple shep-herd,
Pa - sto - rel - lo, sei sog - get - to Fa - cil - men - te a t'in - gan - nar, Pa - sto - rel - lo,

thou art sure-ly Prone thy sen - ses to be-guile, prone thy sen - ses to be-guile.
sei sog - get - to Fa - cil - men - te a t'in - gan - nar, Fa - cil - men - te a t'in - gan - nar.

NINA

Giovanni Battista Pergolesi

English text by Van A. Christy

Edited by Van A. Christy

glia - te mia Ni - net-ta, ac - ciò non dor-ma più, _____ ac-
wak - en Ni - net-ta, I pray thee sleep no more, _____ I

ciò __ non __ dor - ma più; sve - glia - te __ mia __ Ni - net - ta, sve -
pray __ thee __ sleep no more. A - wak - en __ my __ Ni - net - ta, a

glia - te mia Ni - net - ta, ac - ciò __ non dor - ma __ più.
wak - en __ my Ni - net - ta, I pray __ thee __ sleep no __ more.

più, ac ciò non dor ma più.
more, I pray thee sleep _____ no more.

*Trill optional

FOREST, THY GREEN ARBORS
(Selve, voi che le speranze)

English text by Charles Fonteyn Manney

Salvator Rosa

*Accompaniment realized by Van A. Christy

*Copyright 1926, Oliver Ditson Company. Used by permission.

* Optional

TO BE NEAR THEE
(Star vicino)

Salvator Rosa

English text by Van A. Christy

Edited and Arranged by Van A. Christy

va - go di - let - to d'a - mor!
joy and de - light of my heart.

Star lon -
To be

ta - no dal ben che si bra - ma, È d'a -
far from your own fair be - lov - ed Is the

mo - re il più vi - vo do - lor, È d'a -
deep - est grief love doth im - part, Is the

68

*Upper notes optional

THE SUN O'ER THE GANGES
(Già il sole dal Gange)

Alessandro Scarlatti

English text by Van A. Christy

Edited by Van A. Christy

71

chia - ro sfa - vil - la, più chia - ro, più chia - ro sfa -
gem - ma o - gni ste - lo, in gem - ma o - gni ste - lo, in -
ris - es in splen - dor, the sun - god, the sun - god in
jew - els of sun - light, like jew - els, like jew - els of

vil - la.
ste - lo.
splen - dor.
sun - light.

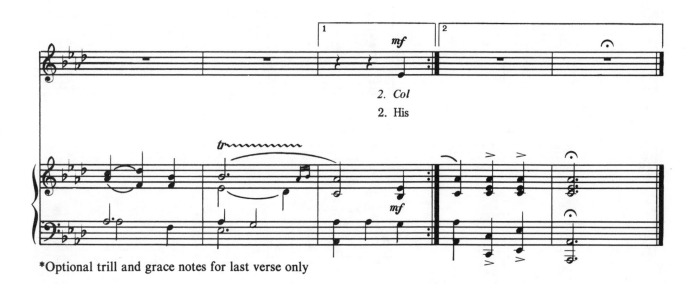

2. Col
2. His

*Optional trill and grace notes for last verse only

WELL THOU KNOWEST
(Tu lo sai)

Giuseppe Torelli

*English text by George Harris

*Modern concert transcription by
Pietro Floridia

*Used by permission of the Oliver Ditson Company, Bryn Mawr, Pa.

ow - est To me burn-ing and yearn-ing in vain.
ma - i, Tu lo sa - i, lo sa - i, cru - del!

Oth - er fa - vors are not my plea,
Io non bra - mo al - tra mer - cé,

But that thou re - mem - ber me,
Ma ri - cor - da - ti di me,

Then as worth - less de-spise a - gain,
E poi sprez - za un in - fe - del,

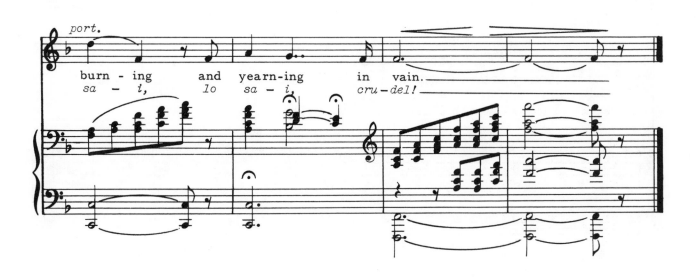

77

WITH CUNNING CONNIVING
(Che fiero costume)

Giovanni Legrenzi

English text by Van A. Christy

Edited and Arranged by Van A. Christy

79

forza di pena si faccia adorar!
drive me by torment his art to adore!

Che
This

crudo destino che un cieco bambino con
winged wee mite, tho' depriv'd of his sight, Scarce

bocca di latte si faccia stimar, si faccia stimar, con
wean'd, yet his arrows assail ev'ry heart, as sail ev'ry heart, Scarce

bocca di latte si faccia stimar!
wean'd, yet his arrows assail ev'ry heart!

80

SAPPHIC ODE
(Sapphische Ode)

Hans Schmidt

Johannes Brahms

English text by Van A. Christy

Edited by Van A. Christy

Ro—sen brach ich nachts mir am dunk—len Ha - ge;
Ro-ses I at night cull from dark-n'ing hedge - rows

sü - sser hauch—ten Duft sie, als je___ am Ta - ge,
Breathe a sweet - er fra - grance than day___ be - stows;___

doch ver - streu—ten reich die be—weg - ten
And the leaf - lets when I dis-turb___ them

83

Ae — ste Thau _____ der mich
throw me Drops _____ to be -

näss — — — te.
dew _____ me.

Auch der Küs — se Duft mich wie nie be — rück — te,
So thy kiss-es fra — grance my heart has sha — ken,

84

die ich nachts vom Strauch dei—ner Lip — pen pflück — te:
Kiss-es I at night from thy lips___ have tak — en;

doch auch dir, be - wegt im Ge—müth___ gleich
And so moved wert thou when my kiss - es

je — nen, thau — — ten die Thrä — —
wooed thee, Tear — — drops be - dew'd___

nen.
me.

TO THE DISTANT BELOVED

(An die ferne Geliebte)

A. Jeitteles

Ludwig van Beethoven

English text by Van A. Christy

*Edited by Van A. Christy

*This song is an excerpt from the song cycle of the same name. The editor has combined the introductory section and its recapitulation at the end of the cycle to provide an art song in complete and satisfactory form.

theilt.
low.

Will den nichts mehr zu dir
Is there no way I can

drin—gen nichts der Lie—be Bo — te sein? Sin—gen will ich, Lie — der
find thee, No far road to love___ re—gain? May my songs fly to___ re—

sin—gen, die dir kla — gen mei—ne Pein!
mind thee Of my lone—li—ness and pain.

Dann vor die — sen Lied—ern
Ah, may then my songs ob—

BY THE SEA
(Am Meer)

Heinrich Heine

English text by Arthur Westbrook
Revised by Van A. Christy

From *Schwanengesang* by
Franz Schubert

Edited by Van A. Christy

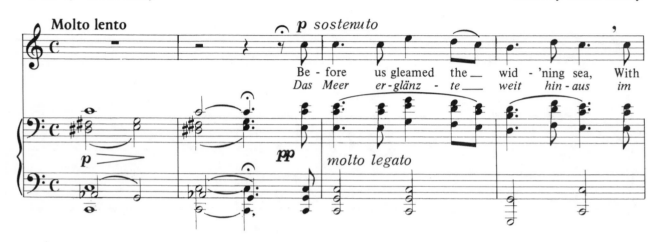

Be - fore us gleamed the __ wid - 'ning sea, With
Das Meer er - glänz - te __ weit hin - aus im

eve's last glow in - vest - ed; We sat in the des - o - late
letz - ten A - bend - schei - ne; wir sas - sen am ein - sa - men

fish - ing hut, A - lone, and si - lent, we rest - ed.
Fisch - er - haus; wir sas - sen stumm und al - lei - ne.

The mist a-rose,   the waves roll'd high,   The
Der Ne - bel stieg,   *das Was - ser schwoll,*   *die*

sea - gull a - round us was sweep - ing;   I gazed up - on_ thy_
Mö - ve flog hin und wie - der;   *aus dei - nen Au - gen_*

love - lit eyes,   Dar - ling, I saw thee weep - ing.   The
lie - be-voll   *fie - len die Thrä - nen nie - der.*   *Ich*

tears fell fast on thy gen - tle hand, And low be - side thee_ kneel - ing, From
sah sie fal - len auf dei - ne Hand, und bin auf's Knie ge - sunk - en; ich

that white hand I kiss'd a-way The tear-drops o'er it steal - ing.
hab' von dein-er weis-sen Hand die Thrä-nen fort ge-trunk - en.

With fa - tal long-ing con-sum'd from that hour, My
Seit je - ner Stun-de ver-zehrt sich mein Leib, die

soul for-spent with yearn - ing; They had, a-las! a pois-'nous
Seel - e stirbt vor Sehn - en; mich hat das un-glück-sel - ge

pow'r, — Those tears on my lips still burn - ing.
Weib — ver - gif-tet mit ihr - en Thrä - nen.

94

HEDGE ROSE
(Heidenröslein)

Johann Wolfgang von Goethe

Franz Schubert

Translator unknown

Edited by Van A. Christy

Con tenerezza (♩ =69)

Once a boy a rose espied, In the hedge-row grow-ing:
Sah ein Knab' ein Rös-lein steh'n, Rös-lein auf der Hei - den,

Fresh in all her youth-ful pride, When her beau-ties he de-scried,
war so jung und mor-gen-schön, lief er schnell, es nah! zu seh'n,

cresc. *p rit.*

Joy in his heart was glow-ing. Lit-tle wild rose, wild rose red,
sah's mit vie-len Freu-den. Rös-lein, Rös-lein, Rös-lein roth,

95

In the hedge-row grow - ing.
Rös-lein auf der Hei - den.

Said the boy, "I'll
Kna - be sprach: „ich

gath - er thee, In the hedge-row grow - ing!" Said the rose, "Then I'll pierce thee
bre - che dich, Rös-lein auf der Hei - den!" Rös-lein sprach: „ich ste - che dich,

That you may re - mem - ber me", Thus re - proof be - stow - ing. Lit - tle wild rose,
dass du e - wig denkst an mich, und ich will's nicht lei - den". Rös-lein, Rös-lein,

wild rose red, In the hedge-row grow - ing.
Rös - lein roth, Rös-lein auf der Hei - den.

IMPATIENCE
(Ungeduld)

Wilhelm Muller

From *Die Schöne Müllerin* by
Franz Schubert

English text by Van A. Christy

Edited by Van A. Christy

1. I'd   carve it deep on   all   the
2. A star - ling young and dear I'll
3. Tho all   too plain it shines with -

1. *Ich schnitt' es gern in al — le*
2. *Ich möcht' mir zie — hen ei — nen*
3. *Ich meint', es musst' in mei — nen*

trees that grow, En-grave it on each stone where e'er I go, I
catch and train Un-til my words of love he'd clear-ly frame, So
in my eyes, In blush-es which up-on my cheeks a-rise, While

Rin-den ein, ich grüb es gern in je-den Kie-sel-stein, ich
jun-gen Starr, bis dass er spräch' die Wor-te rein und klar, bis
Au-gen steh'n, auf mei-nen Wan-gen müsst' mann's bren-nen seh'n. zu

cresc.

fain would sow it in each gar-den green, In ev'-ry plant it shall be
ev'-ry lov-ing word he might im-part Like those a-wak-en'd in my
on my si-lent lips it can be read, With ev'-ry breath I draw 'tis

möcht' es sa'n auf je-des fri-sche Beet, mit Kres-sen-sa-men, der es
er sie spräch' mit mei-nes Mun-des Klang, mit mei-nes Her-zens vol-lem
le-sens war's auf mei-nem stun-men Mund, ein je-der A-them-zug gäb's

cresc.

Meno Mosso

quick-ly seen, And on each page should be in-scribed for-ev-er:
con-stant heart Ah, would he sing it at thy win-dow ev-er:
al-ways said; And yet the love-ly maid hath mark'd it nev-er:

schnell ver-räth, auf je-den wei-ssen Zet-tel möcht es schrei-ben:
hei-ssen Drang, dann säng' er hell durch ih-re Fen-ster schei-ben:
laut ihr kund, und sie merkt nichts von all' dem ban-gen Trei-ben:

Meno Mosso

SERENADE
(Ständchen)

Franz Schubert

English text by Van A. Christy

*Arranged by Van A. Christy

1. Soft-ly floats my song of plead-ing Thro' the night to thee,
1. Lei - se fle - hen mei - ne Lie - der durch die Nacht zu dir,

In the qui - et woods I wait thee,
in die stil - len Hain her - nie - der,

Thro' the night to thee,
durch die Nacht zu dir,

In the qui - et woods I wait thee,
in die stil - len Hain her - nie - der,

*Optional duet or solo for medium or high voice

101

Hear the night - in - gales' sweet sing - ing, Ah, they plead for me,
Hörst die Nach - ti - gal - len schla - gen? Ach! sie fle - hen dich,

With their tones so clear, so ring - ing,
mit der Tö - ne sü - ssen Kla - gen

Ah, they plead for me, With their tones so clear, so ring - ing,
Ach! sie fle - hen dich, mit der Tö - ne sü - ssen Kla - gen

They en - treat with thee.
fle - hen sie für mich.

They en - treat with thee. Ah, they en - treat with thee.
fle - hen sie für mich. Ach, fle - hen sie für mich.

Know they well a lov-er's long-ing, Know the pain to part,
Sie ver-steh'n des Bu-sens Seh-nen, ken-nen Lie-bes-schmerz,

Know they well a lov-er's long-ing,
Sie ver-steh'n des Bu-sens Seh-nen,

Know the pain to part,
ken-nen Lie-bes-schmerz,
With their sil-ver throat-ed voi-ces
rüh-ren mit den Sil-ber-tö-nen

Know the pain to part.
ken-nen Lie-bes-schmerz,
With their sil-ver throat-ed voi-ces
rüh-ren mit den Sil-ber-tö-nen

Calm each ach-ing heart,
je-des wei-che Herz,
Calm each ach-ing heart._____
je-des wei-che Herz._____

Calm each ach-ing heart,
je-des wei-che Herz,
Calm each ach-ing heart._____
je-des wei-che Herz._____

*Optional vocal ending by the arranger not in the original score and intended to be used only in duet form.

I'LL NOT COMPLAIN
(Ich grolle nicht)

Heinrich Heine

Robert Schumann

English text by Van A. Christy

Edited by Van A. Christy

strahlst in Di – a – men–ten–pracht, es fällt kein Strahl in dei – nes
deck'd in dia-mond splen-dor bright, No answ'-ring ray il – lumes thy

Herz – ens Nacht; das weiss ich längst._____
heart's dark night, I know it well._____

a tempo
Ich grol – le nicht und wenn das Herz auch
I'll not com-plain, al-tho' my heart should

bricht. Ich sah dich ja im Trau – me und sah die
break, In dreams I oft be hold thee, and see re-

Nacht in dei — nes Her — zens Rau — me,   und sah die
morse with - in its toils en - fold thee,   The ser - pent

cresc.

*Schlang' die' dir am Her — zen frisst,_____ ich sah, mein
dread gnaw at thy faith - less heart,_____ Now all for -

cresc.   **ff**   *rit.*

a tempo   *rit.*   **f** *a tempo*   *rit.*

Lieb, wie sehr du e — lend bist.   Ich grol - le nicht,   ich grol - le
lorn and wretch-ed lone thou art.   I'll not com-plain,   I'll not com-

a tempo   *rit.*   *a tempo*   *rit.*

*nicht.*_____
plain._____
a tempo

ff   **f f f**

*High part indicated as optional by composer.

110

TOMORROW
(Morgen)

John Henry Mackay

English text by John Bernhoff
Revised by Van A. Christy

Richard Strauss

Edited by Van A. Christy

Und mor—gen wird die
To-mor-row's sun will

Son — ne wie — der schei —nen und auf dem We — ge, den ich
rise in glor — y beam-ing, and in the path — way that my

ge - hen wer - de, wird uns, die Glück-li-chen sie wie - der ei -
foot shall wan-der, we'll meet in joy-ful-ness, and lost in dream-

- nen in-mit - ten die-ser son - nen at - men-den Er - de
- ing, let heav'n u-nite a love that earth no more shall sun-der

und zu dem Strand, dem wei - ten, wo-gen blau-en, wer - den wir
and towards that shore, it's bil - lows soft-ly flow-ing, our hands en-

still und lang-sam nie-der stei-gen,
twined, our foot-steps slow-ly wend-ing,

112

I DREAMED THAT I WAS WEEPING

(Ich hab' im Traum geweinet)

Heinrich Heine

Robert Schumann

English text by Van A. Christy

Edited by Van A. Christy

Ich hab' im Traum ge — wei — net, / mir
I dreamed that I was weep — ing, / I

träum — te du lä — gest im Grab. / Ich wach — te auf, und die
dreamed in the grave you were laid. / Then I a — woke and the

Thrä — ne / floss noch von der Wan — ge her — ab. / Ich
tear — drops Still ____ down my wan ____ cheek stray'd. / I

hab' im Traum ge – wei – net,
dreamed that I was weep-ing,
mir

träumt!, du ver – lie – ssest mich.
cause you were false to me.
Ich wach-te auf, und ich
Then I a-woke and re-

wein – te noch lan – ge bit – ter-lich.
memb'-ring, Wept long and bit-ter-ly.

Ich hab' im Traum ge – wei – net, mir
I dreamed that I was weep – ing, I

TO YOU
(Zueignung)

Hermann von Gilm

Richard Strauss

English text by Van A. Christy

Edited by Van A. Christy

Ja,   du weisst es,
Ah,   my dear - est,

theu - re See - le,   dass ich fern von dir___ mich quä - le,
sor - rows grieve me,   Far from you my   life___ is gloo - my,

Lie - be macht   die Her - zen krank,   *ha - be*
Part - ing mak - eth sick the   heart: Thanks, dear

119

ALL SOULS' DAY
(Allerseelen)

Hermann von Gilm

Richard Strauss

Translated by Van A. Christy

Edited by Van A. Christy

Stell' auf den
Un - to me

Tisch die duf - ten - den Re - se - den, *die*
bring the glow - ing pur - ple hea - ther, The

letz- ten ro- then A- stern trag' her- bei,
last red as- ters bring to me to day,
und lass uns
And let us

wie- der von der Lie — be re — den,
speak a- gain of love to- geth- er,
wie
As

einst im Mai.
once in May.

Gib mir die Hand, dass ich sie heim-lich drü-cke,
Place thy dear hand in mine in sweet sur-ren-der,

und wenn man's sieht,_____ mir ist es ei–ner–lei, gib mir nur ei–nen
Tho' oth-ers see,_____ I care not what they say; Give me one glance, love,

dei – ner sü – ssen Bli – cke, wie einst im
fond and warm and ten – der, As once in

Mai.
May.

Es blüht und duf – tet heut auf
There blooms to - day_____ on ev'- ry

je – – dem Gra – be, ein Tag im Jahr ist ja den
grave_____ a flow - er, Sa - cred to death are all the

122

SECRECY
(Verborgenheit)

Eduard Mörike

Hugo Wolf

Translator unknown
English text revised by Van A. Christy

Edited by Van A. Christy

Slowly and with great feeling ($\quarternote$=60)

Lass, o Welt, o lass mich sein!
Lure me not, O World, a - gain,

lo—cket nicht mit Lie— bes ga—ben, lasst dies Herz al—lei—ne ha—ben
Tempt me not with joys that per-ish, Let my heart, un-spo - ken, cher-ish

sei — ne Won — — ne, sei - ne Pein!
All its rap - - ture, all its pain.

Was ich trau—re,
Un - known grief con-

124

weiss ich nicht,_____ es ist un – be – kann – tes We – he;
sumes my days,_____ 'Tis with eyes all veiled by sor – row,

im – mer – dar durch Thrä – nen se – he ich der Son – ne
That, when dawns each hope – less mor – row, On the glo – rious

lie – bes Licht.
sun I gaze.

with increasing passion

Oft bin ich mir
On – ly dream – ing

and animation

kaum be – wusst,_____ und die hel – le Freu – de zü – cket
brings me rest,_____ On – ly then a ray of glad – ness

125

durch die Schwe—re, so mich drü—cket, won — nig—lich in mei—ner
Sent from Hea—ven, cheers my sad—ness, Lights the gloom with—in my

Brust. Lass, o Welt, o lass mich sein!
breast. Lure me not, O World, a — gain,

lo — cket nicht mit Lie — bes ga — ben, lasst dies Herz al —
Tempt me not with joys that per — ish, Let my heart, un —

lei — ne ha — ben sei — ne Won — ne, sei — ne Pein!
spo — ken, cher—ish All its rap — ture, all its pain!

EVENING FAIR
(Beau Soir)

Paul Bourget

Claude Debussy

English text by Van A. Christy

Edited by Van A. Christy

Oft in the set-ting sun   wa-ters glow like red
Lorsque au so-leil cou — chant   les ri — viè — res sont

ro — ses,   And a shim — mer-ing trem-or waves o'er fields of
ro — ses,   Et qu'un tiè — de fris — son court sur les champs de

bloom, _____ For we shall all de-part,
beau, _____ Car nous nous en al-lons,

like yon-der wat-er flow-ing To dis-tant
com me s'en va cette on-de Elle à la

seas, _____ While we to the
mer, _____ nous au tom -

tomb. _____
beau. _____

129

AFTER A DREAM

(Après un rêve)

From *The Tuscan* by
Romain Bussine

Gabriel Fauré

English text by Van A. Christy

Edited by Van A. Christy

Once while in sleep_____that your vi - sion did
Dans un som - meil_____que char - mait ton i-

fash - ion, I was dream-ing of love and ar-dent pas - -
ma - ge, Je rê-vais le bon-heur ar-dent mi - ra - -

sion; How glow-ing were thine eyes,___thy voice soft and ten - der,
ge; Tes yeux é - taient plus doux,___ta voix pure et so-no - re,

All ra - diant thou as the sky_____ at Au - ro - ra's sur-
Tu ray - on - nais comme un ciel_____ é-clai - ré par l'au -

ren - der. I heard you
ro - re; Tu m'ap - pe -

call_____ and in dream it was giv - en To de - part from this
lais_____ et je quit-tais la ter - re Pour m'en-fuir a - vec

land with thee to Heav - - en;
toi vers la lu - miè - - re;

Heav'n then—re—vealed—its se—cret splen—dor, Un—
Les cieux—pour—nous en—tr'ou—vraient leurs nu—es, Splen—

dream'd—of joy—did ren—der, Vi—sions of glo—ry, deep and
deurs—in—con—nu—es, Lu—eurs di—vi—nes en—tre—

ten—der. A—las! a—las! Sad 'tis that dreams—soon
vu—es. Hé—las! Hé—las, tris—te ré—veil—des

fade——a—way, That the night must
son——ges, Je t'ap—pel—le, ô

end——— all joy in the cru — — el day! Re -
nuit,——— rends-moi tes men—son — — ges, Re -

turn, re — turn ra - diant dream -
viens, re — viens ra — di — eu — —

ing, Re - turn, Oh, night's mys - ter - ious
se, Re — viens, ô nuit mys — té — ri —

seem — — — — ing!
eu — — — — sel

133

THE CRADLES
(Les Berceaux)

Sully Prudhomme

Gabriel Fauré

*English text by Noble Cain

Edited by Van A. Christy

Andantino (♩.=72)

Legato, with swaying motion

con Pedale

Le long du quai,_____ les grands_vais-seaux Que la hou-le in-cli-ne-en si - len - ce,_____ Ne pre - nant pas gar - de aux_____ ber-ceaux,

A - long the quay,_____ with sails_____ a - loft, Gal-lant ships with waves round them play - ing,_____ For- get, in their pride,_____ the cra - dles soft

*Copyright 1933–1938 by Hall & McCreary Company. Used by permission.

*Optional part recommended for low female voice.

135

137

FLORIAN'S SONG
(Chanson de Florian)

J. P. Claris de Florian

Benjamin Godard

English text by Laura M. Underwood

Edited by Van A. Christy

THE EXQUISITE HOUR
(L'Heure exquise)

Paul Verlaine

Reynaldo Hahn

English text by Van A. Christy

Edited by Van A. Christy

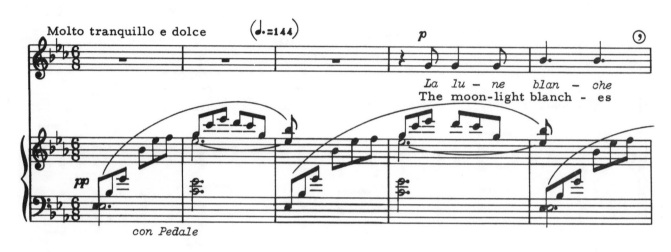

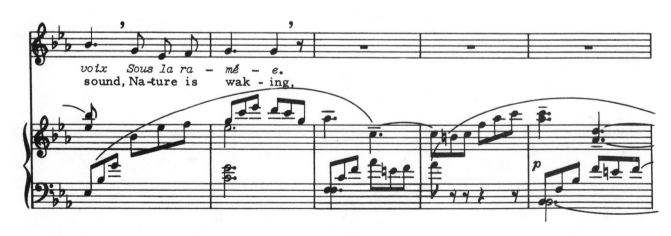

cen - dre Du fir - ma - ment Que l'astre i - ri - se.
fades____ in heav-n'ly light, The stars are gleam - ing.

C'est
Oh,

l'heu - re ex - qui - - - se.
love - ly hour _____ of dream - ing!

WERE MY SONGS WITH WINGS PROVIDED
(Si mes vers avaient des ailes)

Victor Hugo

Reynaldo Hahn

English text by Theodore Baker

Edited by Van A. Christy

Mes vers fui-raient, doux et frê-les,
My song would fly, all un-aid-ed,

Vers vo-tre jar-din si beau
To thy gar-den at a word,

Si mes vers a-
Were my song with

vaient des ai-les
wings pro-vid-ed,

Com-me l'oi-seau!
Like to a bird!

147

I WEPT, BELOVED, AS I DREAMED
(J'ai pleuré en rêve)

*Gerard de Nerval

Georges Hüe

**English text by Carl Engel

Edited by Van A. Christy

*After the German of Heinrich Heine

**Used by permission of the Boston Music Co.

lè – rent de mes jou – es. J'ai pleu – ré en
eyes a burn-ing flood of tears. I wept be –

rê – ve; J'ai rê – vé que tu me qui – tais;
lov ed, as I dreamed thou hadst for-sak – en me;

Je m'é – veil – lai, ___ et je pleu – rai a – mè – re –
And when I woke ___ I sobbed and cried all the gray

ment long – temps a – près. J'ai pleu – ré en
morn, my love, for thee. I wept, Be –

THE CAPTIVE
(L'Esclave)

Théophile Gautier

Édouard Lalo

English text by Van A. Christy

Edited by Van A. Christy

ti - ve,_____ et peut-ê - tre ou - bli - é - e, Je
cap - tive,_____ and per - chance long for got - ten, I

songe__à mes jeu - nes a - mours,_____ À mes beaux jours!_____
dream__of my young love of yore,_____ Of days no more!_____

à mes beaux jours!
of days no more!

Et par la fe–nê–tre gril–
And through a cap-tive's

lé — e   Je re-gar – de l'oi-seau joy-eux fen-dant les cieux!
win – dow,   See a-rise The joy - ous bird wing thro' the skies!

Au – près de lui,
Ah, ra - diant hope,

a tempo   senza respiare

rit.   a tempo

belle es – pé – ran – ce,   Por – te–moi sur tes
hast - en to bear   me   near to him on your

ai – les d'or, _____ S' il m' aime en – core, _____
wings of gold, _____ Lest love be cold,

_____ S' il m' aime en – core! _____
Lest love be cold!

Et pour en–dor–mir ma souf–fran – – ce, Sus –
And soothe my sor–row and griev – – ing, Lay

pens mon â – me sur son coeur _____ Comme u–ne fleur!
on his heart _____ my soul, my all, _____ As flow–ers fall!

ELEGY
(Élégie)

Louis Gallet

Jules Massenet

English text by Van A. Christy

Edited by Van A. Christy

vain que re-vient le prin-temps! Oui sans re-tour, a-vec toi
me doth the spring-time re-turn! Ah, gone for-ev-er with thee,

le gai so-liel,
Dark is the sun!
Les jours ri-ants sont par-tis! Comme en mon
Days full of laugh-ter have fled. Cold is my

coeur tout est sombre et gla-cé Tout est flé-tri!_____
heart and as dark as the tomb! Now all is dead,_____

Pour tou-jours!_____
ev - - er more!_____

ABIDE WITH ME
(Bist du bei mir)

Melody and Bass by
Johann Sebastian Bach

English text by Van A. Christy

Piano accompaniment by Van A. Christy

Then go I glad - ly To death and ev-er-last - ing
Geh' ich mit Freu - den zum Ster-ben und zu mein-er

peace, to _____ death and ev-er-last-ing peace. Ah, how con -
Ruh', zum _____ Ster-ben und zu mein-er Ruh'. Ach wie ver-

tent Would be my end - ing, If I _____ could
gnügt wär' so mein En - de: Es drück-ten_____

feel Thy gen - tle_____ fin-gers laid soft-ly on my clos-ing eyes.
dei-ne schon-end'_____ Hän-de mir die ge-treu-en Au-gen zu.

*Trill is optional

158

O DIVINE REDEEMER
(Repentir)

Charles Gounod

*Edited by Van A. Christy

Ah!___ ne re-pous-se pas___ mon â - me pé-che-res - se!
Ah!___ Turn me not a - way,___ re - ceive me, tho' un - wor - thy!

*Optional duet or solo for medium or high voice by following the melody line

160

161

162

170

O LOVELY PEACE

From *Judas Maccabaeus* by
George Frederick Handel

*Edited and Arranged by Van A. Christy

*Optional duet or solo for medium or high voice by following the melody line

171

172

174

*There is piano accompaniment only for two measures when sung as a solo.

*Trills may be omitted if desired.

O SLEEP, WHY DOST THOU LEAVE ME

William Congreve

From *Semele* by
George Frederick Handel

Edited by Van A. Christy

*Trill optional for flexible voices.

vi-sion-a-ry joys re - move? _____ O _____ Sleep, O ___

Sleep,   O Sleep, a-gain de-ceive me,   O Sleep a-gain de-ceive me, To   my

arms   re - store my wan - d'ring love,   My wan - - -

(Ossia) My wan - - -

- d'ring love,   my ___

O LORD, HAVE MERCY

(Pietá, Signore)

Alessandro Stradella

English text by Van A. Christy

Edited by Van A. Christy

181

se a te giun - ge_il mi - o pre - gar; Non mi pu -
Show me Thy fa - vor, heed___ my___ pray'r. Lord God in

ni - sca_il tu - o ri - gor, Me - no se - ve - ri,
mer - cy hear___ my___ call, Be an - gry nev - er,

cle - men - ti_o - gno - ra, Vol - gi_i tuo - i sguar - di so - pra di
for - giv - ing ev - er, Shine Thy light up - on me, Lest I should

me, so pra_di - me. Non___ fi - a___ ma - i
fall, lest I___ should fall! Lord, I___ im - plore_Thee,

*All vocal trills optional

*optional

185

WEEP NO MORE

From *Hercules* by
George Frederick Handel

Edited by Van A. Christy

Larghetto e sostenuto (♩=56)

Weep no more, weep no more, nor

sigh, nor groan, nor sigh, nor groan,

186

Sor - row re - calls no time _____ that's gone; Vio - lets

plucked, the sweet - est rain Makes not fresh nor grow a -

gain, nor grow _____ a - gain.

Joys as wing - ed dreams _ fly _ fast, Why should sad - ness,

Joys as wing - ed dreams fly_____ fast,

Why should sad - ness long - er last?

Why, why,

why, why should sad - ness long - er last?

LEAVE ME TO LANGUISH
(Lascia ch'io pianga)

From *Rinaldo* by
George Frederick Handel

*English text by John S. Dwight

Edited by Van A. Christy

*Used by permission of the Oliver Ditson Co., Bryn Mawr, Pa.

190

tor - men - to so_in - fer - no! Si - gnor! deh'! per pie -
tor - ment all in - fer - nal, O Heav'n! for pit - y's

tà, Las - cia - mi pian - ge - re!
sake, Let this poor heart soon break.

Largo (♩=63)

con 8va

pp sostenuto

Las - cia ch'io pian - ga mia cru - da sor - te, E che so -
Leave me to lan - guish A - lone with sor - row, Weep - ing and

191

192

Il duo - lo_in-fran - ga   Ques - te ri - tor - te
Long night of an - guish! Come soon, O mor - row,

De' miei mar - ti - ri Sol per pie - tà,___ si,
With hope_ re - turn - ing, This heart to   cheer,__ ah,

De'___ miei___ mar - ti - ri Sol per - pie - tà.
With ___ hope ___ re - turn - ing, This heart to   cheer.

*Trill optional

193

O DEATH NOW COME
(Lasciatemi morire)

From *Arianna* by
Claudio Monteverdi

English text by Van A. Christy

*Edited by Van A. Christy

*Used by permission of the Oliver Ditson Co., Bryn Mawr, Pa.

che mi con - for - te in co - sì du - ra
Could stay one mo - ment My des - pair and my

sor - te, in co - sì gran mar -
tor - ment in such a mar - tyr's

ti - re? La - scia - te - mi mo - ri - re,
an - guish? O Death now come to save me!

La - scia - te - mi mo - ri - re!
O Death now come to save me!

195

DIDO'S LAMENT

From *Dido and Aeneas* by
Henry Purcell

Edited by Van A. Christy

wrongs_____cre - ate no trou - ble, no trou - ble in thy_____

breast. Re - mem-ber me, re -

mem-ber me, But ah!_____for-get my

fate; Re mem-ber me, but ah!_____for-get my fate; Re -

mem-ber me,   re - mem-ber me, But ah! _____for-get my

fate;   Re - mem-ber me,   but   ah! _____for - get my ___fate!

AH, POOR HEART!

(Ah! mio cor)

From *Alcina* by
George Frederick Handel

Edited by Van A. Christy from
the Alessandro Parisotti setting

*English text by Theodore Baker

Andante stretto ($\bullet$=104)

Ah,_____ poor__ heart!
*Ah!*_____ *mio__ cor,*

(she)
he scorns thy love._____
*scher—ni—to se—i.*_____

Hear me,
Stel—le,

*Used by permission of G. Schirmer, Inc., holders of the original copyright.

weep-ing and lone-ly,   canst thou leave me, O   Heav-en! and
so — la   in pian-to,   puoi la — sciar-mi, oh   De — i,   per-

why?
che?

Ah,   poor   heart!_____ (she) he scorns thy love.____   Hear   me,___
Ah!   mio   co — re,   scher — ni-to se — i.___   Stel — le,___

Heav - en,   ye gods a - bove!_____   Thee,   O
De — i,   Nu — me d'a-mo — re!___   tra — di-

trai - tor,   love I on - ly,   Canst thou leave me weep-ing,
to - re,   t'a - mo tan - to,   puoi la-sciar—mi sola in

lone - ly,   O Heav - en!   Canst _____ thou _____
pian - to,   oh De - i,   puo - i la

leave me   weep-ing,   weep-ing,   weep-ing,   lone - ly,
sciar—mi   so - la,   so - la,   so—la in   pian—to,

canst thou leave me, O   Heav-en!   and why?   and
puoi la sciar—mi, oh   De - i,   per - chè?   per—

why?   and why?   Canst thou leave me weep-ing, lone-ly,   O
chè?   per-chè?   puoi la-sciar-mi so-la in pian-to,   oh

Heav-en!   Canst thou leave me, O   Heav-en,   and why?
De - i!   puoi la - sciar-mi, oh De - i,   per-chè?

Appendix 1   Suggestions for Interpretation

Basic guides to expression—style, tone color, and mood—are given for each song. The recommendations given in this regard are generalizations. Style seldom changes within a song, mood sometimes changes temporarily, and tone color fluctuates considerably in romantic and modern music to express word meaning and emotion. Fluctuation of tone color occurs less frequently in Classic literature.

We must recognize, of course, that there is often more than one way to interpret beautifully a particular song. However, interpretations normally differ in minor detail and not in the fundamentals of basic style, tone color, and mood. Unless a sound reason exists for change, follow the suggestions and the editing in the scores regarding interpretation. They represent a carefully considered, proven, standard way and are valuable guides to effective expression.

Old English and Nineteenth Century English

Anonymous: HAVE YOU SEEN BUT A WHITE LILLIE GROW, p. 6

Style—lyric

Tone color—normal

Mood—reminiscence

The composer of this early seventeenth-century song, one of the most charming in Old English song literature, is unknown. This song, with its simple chordal accompaniment, was revolutionary at the time since contrapuntal writing was still prevalent in England. It is easy and should be sung simply, without any dramatics or loud dynamics, and with an emphasis on clear-cut articulation of the quaint Old English text. The first phrase, ending with an octave upward-scale in 16th notes, makes an excellent exercise for developing agility technic.

Arne: BLOW, BLOW, THOU WINTER WIND, p. 8

Style—lyric

Tone color—normal

Mood—philosophical

Although a century separates this and the previous song, "Have You Seen But a White Lillie Grow," the two have much in common in style. Dr. Arne, the greatest English composer of the eighteenth century, wrote operas, oratorios, and songs. As a writer of songs, his settings of lyrics by Shakespeare, of which this is one, are especially outstanding. With a range of an octave and a third and some wide 7th and octave leaps, it is somewhat more difficult than the previous song mentioned. It makes an outstanding choice as a study assignment for developing evenness of scale involving wide intervals. Sing it straightforwardly with clear-cut diction and a clear tone. Begin the second verse somewhat louder than the first.

Arne: THE LASS WITH THE DELICATE AIR, p. 10

Style—lyric legato, narrative

Tone color—normal

Mood—admiration

The first verse of this delicately graceful song should be sung quite straightforwardly in tempo with only a very slight *ritardando* before the climax at the end. In the second verse, broaden the *ritardando* and emphasize the *fermata* at the climax. Start the third verse somewhat slower and sing it with more intimacy in style. The fourth verse should start with more vigorous tempo and dynamics. A *crescendo* ending *forte* may be used at the *fermata*, if preferred to the *diminuendo* ending indicated, but be sure that the last two measures are sung with great delicacy and finesse. Diction throughout should be crystalline.

Bishop: LOVE HAS EYES, p. 3

> Style—lyric staccato, florid
>
> Tone color—bright
>
> Mood—delighted

"Love Has Eyes" has long been a concert favorite for flexible voices, especially for sopranos. It is an excellent study song for all voices in the introduction and development of a light staccato and florid style. The diction should be crisp and precise, the tempo lively, and the mood light and happy. Contrast the *dolce* section by singing it more slowly, softly, and with a more mellow tone. The indicated optional carry-over of the last phrase of the *dolce* section into the final return of the "A" section is excellent style and recommended for singers with sufficient breath control. Observe the alternating legato portamentos and staccato notes of the ending section for the best effect. Omit the optional trill at the end unless it can be done well.

Carey: A PASTORAL, p. 14

> Style—lyric legato, florid
>
> Tone color—normal to bright
>
> Mood—light and sprightly

This sprightly song offers an easy introduction to florid singing on the "ah" passage. Be sure to sing the grace notes and all other noted in this passage *a tempo*, with rhythmic precision and accuracy of pitch. These eight measures make an excellent flexibility exercise, which may be transposed into various keys. Keep the tone throughout this song light and joyful.

Monro: MY LOVELY CELIA, p. 26

> Style—lyric legato
>
> Tone color—bright
>
> Mood—affectionate admiration

Tenors and baritones particularly favor this song in concert. Keep the sentiment tender and intimate, the *legato* flowing, and work particularly for an especially soft and clear *mezza voce pianissimo* on the phrase, "as soft as air." End the last two measures of the last verse with a pronounced *ritard* and a long *diminuendo* on the word "arms." The last two measures provide an excellent exercise for this technic.

Morley: IT WAS A LOVER AND HIS LASS, p. 16

> Style—accented
>
> Tone color—normal
>
> Mood—joyous

Thomas Morley, an outstanding English composer of the sixteenth century, is best known for his contrapuntal madrigal writing; "It Was a Lover and His Lass" is well known in its Morley madrigal setting. It is also heard frequently as a solo—usually with Granville Bantock's arrangement, to which I have added a short introduction and a different ending in the fourth verse to provide more finality. Except for the one phrase marked *legato*, sing this with a joyous lilt and an accented style. Emphasize the story with clear-cut articulation in a straightforward, simple manner without bombast on the *forte* climaxes.

Purcell: COME UNTO THESE YELLOW SANDS, p. 18

> Style—florid legato, staccato in last section
>
> Tone color—bright
>
> Mood—happy

The song is marked carefully for dynamic contrast on the repeat of sections. Be sure to keep the accented notes short in the last section. This is both an excellent concert song and a fine study for developing flexibility.

Purcell: I ATTEMPT FROM LOVE'S SICKNESS TO FLY, p. 20

Style—lyric legato, florid

Tone color—normal

Mood—contemplative

Sing this song with a light touch; crisp articulation; a clear, free bel canto tone; and careful attention to the phrasing characteristic of the Old English style. It is an excellent study song to improve agility and introduce florid style. The text is simple in meaning— the inability to escape from the clutches of Cupid—however, it is phrased in the Old English idiom. Proper style is absolutely necessary to bring out its unusual "flavor." Sing the contrasting "B" and "C" sections with somewhat more force, warmth of tone, and slower tempo—although no part of the song can be sung with heavy-handed dramatics. The piano accompaniment should be fluid and light.

Quilter: NOW SLEEPS THE CRIMSON PETAL, p. 24

Style—lyric legato

Tone color—bright

Mood—loving reminiscence

Roger Quilter is ranked as one of the most gifted English song composers of his century. A number of his charming and beautifully constructed songs can be programmed today in any serious art song concert without apology. This song and "Weep You No More, Sad Fountains," have much in common. Both songs are in the minor mode, have fine texts, and hauntingly beautiful melodies that are memorable. The text of "Now Sleeps the Crimson Petal" is by Tennyson. At first glance, this song may appear forbidding and difficult, because of its shifting back and forth between 3/4 and 5/4 meters; however, the melody flows naturally without any feeling of irregularity. Sing it with a clear, plaintive tone, emphasizing purity of vowels, clear tone, even scale, smooth phrasing, and control of indicated dynamics.

Quilter: WEEP YOU NO MORE, SAD FOUNTAINS, p. 29

Style—lyric legato

Tone color—bright

Mood—philosophical, sad memorial

Read the previous analysis of "Now Sleeps the Crimson Petal," since "Weep You No More, Sad Fountains" is sung in a similar fashion. The text is especially suitable for *pianissimo* singing. Quilter's setting realizes its full potential. The range of this outstanding song is only a 9th, but other demands of interpretation make it a song of moderate difficulty.

Sullivan: ORPHEUS WITH HIS LUTE, p. 32

Style—lyric legato with some long sustained notes

Tone color—normal to bright

Mood—happy

Although not an Old English song, "Orpheus With His Lute" is placed under this heading as its best position in this song anthology. It is remarkable that this outstanding song with a Shakespearian text has not become more popular with concert singers. It has spontaneity and lilt in the melody and an interesting art-song type of accompaniment with the reiterated bass figures characteristic of many of the fine Schubert songs. For effective rendition, maintain the *allegro moderato* tempo. Sing lyrically with careful attention to pure, free tone, clear diction, and adequate breath support for the long sustained tones. Two phrases with long sustained *crescendo*—"Everything that heard him play" and "Orpheus with his lute"—are excellent exercises to develop steady sustained *crescendo*, while the next to the last phrase (with the optional high notes) is unsurpassed as an exercise to develop the *mezzo voce* high range.

Old Italian

Caldara: FAIREST ADORED (Alma del core), p. 44

Style—lyric legato

Tone color—bright

Mood—adoration of beloved

This is an easy, attractive Old Italian song of only a 7th in range. Sing it in typical lyric bel canto style. Do not let the tempo drag and do not overemphasize the *forte* climaxes, especially when they are found in the lower voice compass. Not forcing, but gentleness and gracefulness are the required styles for best effect.

Caldara: WHEN ON THE SURGING WAVE (Come raggio di sol), p. 48

> Style—sustained legato
>
> Tone color—normal to dark
>
> Mood—contemplative sorrow

Sustained *legato* and smooth control of *crescendo* and *diminuendo* are needed, although this is not a difficult song to sing effectively. Sing the last phrase, "And bitter, fearful sorrow," with emotional intensity.

Carissimi: VICTORIOUS, MY HEART IS! (Vittoria, mio core!), p. 39

> Style—alternately accented and lyric
>
> Tone color—normal
>
> Mood—vigorous exultation

This song is one of the top concert and recital favorites, especially for a strong, resonant male voice. It is also excellent as an assignment to develop accented technic. The requirements of an octave and a fourth in range, the alternate accented and lyric styles, a fine agility passage on the phrase, "E sciolta d'Amore", and the dynamics from *p* to *f*, make this a song of moderate difficulty, but it is well worth the effort to master it. Observe a rapid tempo to achieve the required mood.

Durante: VIRGIN, FOUNT OF LOVE (Vergin, tutto amor), p. 52

> Style—sustained legato
>
> Tone color—bright
>
> Mood—worship

It should not be forgotten that this is a compassionate prayer, a eulogy to the Virgin Mother, a sinner's plea for mercy. Therefore, no loud *fortissimos* or dramatics are suitable. Sing this song with maximum sustained *legato,* delivering the text of this superb song with sympathetic insight and dynamic restraint as indicated by the intensity markings on the score. A *molto ritard* and an anticipated *portamento* are most effective in the last phrase if done smoothly.

Giordani: DEAR LOVE OF MINE (Caro mio ben), p. 55

> Style—sustained legato
>
> Tone color—normal to bright
>
> Mood—tender affection, sadness from separation

This easy Old Italian song undoubtedly ranks as number one in the preference of beginning students, judging from the number of times it is heard in recitals. It is a superlative study song and a favorite of many teachers as an introduction for the beginning student to the Old Italian song literature. Do not neglect the grace notes near the end. Practice the optional turn in the third measure from the end until it can be done gracefully, and develop sufficient breath energy and control to accomplish the carry-over at the last return of the "A" section with a smooth *diminuendo* and a light *portamento*.

Legrenzi: WITH CUNNING CONNIVING (Che fiero costume), p. 78

> Style—narrative accented
>
> Tone color—normal
>
> Mood—jolly, robust

In spite of a text better suited to female than to male voices, this song is heard more often in concert sung by men. It is unique in style among the Old Italian songs, demanding a fast tempo and a very rapid delivery of the text similar to the Gilbert and Sullivan patter songs. However, it differs from the style of the patter song in that *a good tone and some semblance of legato must be maintained*. No finer study in rapid articulation can be found in all song literature. Study it until the tempo can be maintained as fast or faster than indicated without destroying good tone and clear-cut articulation on each word and syllable. Most amateur accompanists cannot read this song at the required speed and should be urged to practice it assiduously before rehearsals.

Pergolesi: IF THOU LOV'ST ME (Se tu m'ami), p. 58

Style—lyric legato

Tone color—normal

Mood—flirtatious discussion

This unusual and attractive Old Italian song can be sung either as a solo or as a duet, with a female voice singing the first and last parts and a male voice the second. As a duet, it is an easy song for the male voice and also for the female voice that has a usable range of an octave and a fifth. In any case, it should either be sung in the English translation or have a well-considered translation supplied to most English-speaking audiences beforehand or the charm of the repartee and the humorous text will be lost. Keep the tempo moving. A *rubato tempo* in places and a somewhat broader *rit.* than for the typical Old Italian song is recommended in interpreting this song.

Pergolesi: NINA, p. 62

Style—lyric legato with a touch of florid

Tone color—bright

Mood—gentle chiding, affection

"Nina" is a universal favorite, especially with male singers. Repetition of the first section *pianissimo* will provide effective contrast. Sing the first section with a very lyric sustained *legato* and the first phrase of the second section in accented style. If taken in its entirety, the last phrase is an excellent study in breath control and the turn fine for practice of this ornamentation.

Rosa: FOREST, THY GREEN ARBORS (Selve, voi che le speranze), p. 64

Style—lyric legato

Tone color—bright

Mood—peaceful soliloquy, love of the forest

This gentle, quiet, very easy song is a favorite of both students and teachers as an introductory study of the Old Italian song. It was recommended more than any other by reviewers and experienced teachers to be included in the new edition. Emphasize steady breath support, pure vowels, and a very lyric and smooth *legato*. Do not make the **mf** climax bombastic or louder than written.

Rosa: TO BE NEAR THEE (Star vicino), p. 66

Style—sustained lyric legato, with a touch of florid

Tone color—bright

Mood—tender affection

Rosa made a number of settings of "Star vicino," which vary considerably in melody and in the extent of florid treatment. This more straightforward and simple setting is a delightful example of the Early Italian Song; it is excellent both for concert and for the development of a free, flexible tone. Just enough scale passage in eighth notes is included to make it an ideal vehicle in this tempo to develop more agility in logy voices. The song is marked carefully for dynamics and phrasing and should present no special problems in interpretation.

Scarlatti: THE SUN O'ER THE GANGES (Già il sole dal Gange), p. 70

Style—accented, except the short legatiss section

Tone color—normal

Mood—vigorous, energetic

For a number of good reasons, this song is perhaps programmed by men in concert and recital more often than any other Old Italian song. A universal favorite of both students and audiences, this vigorous, forthright song is somewhat unusual in style; most other Old Italian songs are *lyric legato* or *lyric sostenuto*. It should be sung lightly accented, with gusto, and at a fairly fast clip. It is also exceptional in another respect among songs originally sung in the Italian language: the English lyrics provided appear to be just as effective as the Italian lyrics.

Torelli: WELL THOU KNOWEST (Tu lo sai), p. 74

Style—sustained lyric legato

Tone color—bright

Mood—Yearning love, complaint

"Tu lo sai" is easy, musically effective, and well liked by both students and audiences. It furnishes an unsurpassed vehicle for the development of pure vowels, soft dynamics, and the maximum sustained *lyric legato* style. The return of the "A" theme after the "B" section should be as soft and *legato* as can be sung. Pure, clear vowel quality and freedom of production is an absolute requirement for effective expression in this song, as it is in all Old Italian *legato* songs.

German Lieder

Beethoven—TO THE DISTANT BELOVED (An die ferne Geliebte), p. 86

Style—sustained legato

Tone color—approaching dark, warm, and rich

Mood—meditation, tender affection

Beethoven's song cycle, *An die ferne Geliebte*, is generally considered his greatest work for solo voice. It was the first and still the most perfect song cycle in respect to unity. However, the work is seldom heard except in its entirety since the sections are knit into one another in such a fashion that a satisfactory and complete song excerpt is difficult to obtain. This problem has been solved by combining the introduction and its recapitulation at the end into a complete and satisfying art song. Although the range is not taxing, this song requires careful study and sympathetic understanding for a fine interpretation. The sentiment is at once simple and tender, yet profound. The tone should be warm and rich; a restrained but deep emotional fervor should be maintained. The accompaniment should be played sensitively and phrasing and the building up of climaxes should be handled carefully.

Brahms: SAPPHIC ODE (Sapphische Ode), p. 83

Style—sustained, legato

Tone color—dark, warm

Mood—tranquility, introspection, tender affection

This short song—with its emphasis on syncopation in the accompaniment, long flowing phrases, lovely chromatic harmony, and finesse in variation of melodic line—is truly characteristic of Brahms's style. It is easier to phrase if sung nearer *moderato* than *lento* tempo, as some outstanding authorities, including Lotte Lehmann, suggest it should be sung. The text of the first verse deals with the beauty and fragrance of roses plucked at night and the second verse compares favorably the kisses taken at night from the lips of a sweetheart with the previous experience. It should be sung quietly, tenderly, with warm emotion, and extreme sustained *legato*.

Schubert: BY THE SEA (Am Meer), p. 92

Style—sostenuto

Tone color—bright

Mood—intense grief and yearning

With a fine poem by Heinrich Heine and a superbly sensitive musical setting, "By the Sea" (Am Meer) is one of Schubert's finest *sostenuto*-style songs. I believe it will be found equally effective to the unprejudiced ear when sung in the English translation provided. With a range of only a 9th, it is an easy song to sing, if the tempo is mistakenly taken faster than marked. However, at the marked *molto lento* tempo, it is not an easy song to sing either technically or interpretively. Long phrases, complicated by soft dynamics and an extremely steady *sostenuto* style, are never easy. In addition, it is essential that diction be quite clear and dramatically projected. It is a song that wears well and improves continually with technical advance and greater interpretive understanding. This song should not be attempted in recital or concert unless a good accompanist is available. While not technically demanding, the piano part is unusually important in its dramatic and emotional content to which the accompanist must be attuned.

Schubert: HEDGE ROSE (Heidenröslein), p. 95

Style—lyric narrative

Tone color—normal

Mood—gentle, light, descriptive narrative

The genius of Schubert can be no better illustrated than by a comparison of the previous song, "By the Sea" (Am Meer), with "Hedge Rose"—they are direct opposites in almost every category. "Hedge Rose" is undoubtedly one of Schubert's most popular songs with both students and audiences. Its straightforward narrative style, simple phrasing, and one-octave range make it an easy and appropriate introduction to German lieder for initial study by beginning students. Both reviewers and colleagues recommended its inclusion in this edition. Most beginning students can sing this song effectively—the key is attention to clear and understandable diction. Do not forget that this is a ballad with an interesting story that must be told effectively. Keep the tempo moving for dragging will kill the song. *Do not slow the last phrase,* and speed up the following two-measure piano finale for an almost flippant effect.

Schubert: IMPATIENCE (Ungeduld), p. 98

Style—dramatic and rhapsodic

Tone color—normal to bright on the climax

Mood—exultant joy, pride and happiness

Franz Schubert, who composed some six hundred songs, perfected the song as an art form, combining the voice part and accompaniment to produce the highest unity of expression. This song, from the song cycle *Die schöne Müllerin,* is one of his finest, a favorite of both audiences and concert artists. It has an unsurpassed rhapsodic character and literally blossoms into a resounding climax on the third measure from the end. Start quietly and build with a gradual increase in dynamics and emotional fervor to the climax of the third, or last, verse.

Schubert: SERENADE (Ständchen), p. 101

Style—lyric legato

Tone color—bright and pure

Mood—tender love

A favorite love song, "Serenade" should be sung with a flowing tonal quality. Always maintain the emotional fervor even in the quiet passages. Sing the contrasting "B" section somewhat faster and with more tonal force. "Come and bring me joy" (marked *forte*) is the emotional climax and should have an intensity of joyful feeling in the tone. Repeat this phrase quietly at the end in the augmented rhythm like a grateful benediction. This passage requires very steady and sustained breath support as do the longer rhythm notes throughout.

Schumann: I DREAMED THAT I WAS WEEPING (Ich hab'im Traum geweinet), p. 114

Style—sostenuto and semirecitative, dramatic

Tone color—bright, but with a round intense quality, not shrill

Mood—reflective, bitter grief

Although the melody is often *a cappella* and the accompaniment is sketchy, do not mistake the style for free recitative. Take no liberty with the note values indicated. Except for the *crescendo* at the ending phrase, sing the song softly. Maintain the intense but subdued emotional feeling until the last phrase when bitter grief breaks forth in a cry of anguish. Sing the second phrase with dark tone quality. The mood of almost unbearable anguish requires the maintenance of intense emotional feeling. While the accompaniment is sparse, every note must be played eloquently to achieve proper expression. This song is made by the interpretation and neither the singer not the accompanist can "let down" at any time.

Schumann: I'LL NOT COMPLAIN (Ich grolle nicht), p. 108

Style—dramatic

Tone color—variable

Mood—intense sorrow

From a near normal tone quality at the beginning of this magnificent dramatic song, the voice should gradually develop intensity until it reaches a climax in brilliance with the *fortissimo* dynamic climax of the last page. Care must be exercised that neither the tonal brilliance nor the extent of the *fortissimo* is carried beyond capability for good tone; the climax must be neither shouted nor shrieked. Each time the phrase, "I'll not complain," is repeated more softly, the repeat should be accompanied by a darker tone quality.

Strauss: ALL SOULS' DAY (Allerseelen), p. 120

Style—sustained legato

Tonal color—dark and warm

Mood—reminiscently tender, fervent longing at the end

It is well worth the time and effort of both the singer and the accompanist to understand and master this beautiful song. While the vocal line is not especially taxing in range, it requires much subtle finesse both for sudden dynamic and for tone color changes. The accompaniment is not easy in respect to musical phrasing, sustained *legato,* and the reading of low ledger lines. This song begins with restraint and ends with an outburst of passionate longing on the phrase, ''Come to my heart that I may hold thee ever.'' Sing the following *forte* phrase, ''as once in May,'' broadly with bright tone color and abandon, and sing the repetition, which ends the song, quietly, *mezza voce,* like a sigh of remembrance. Sing the two phrases marked *pianissimo* in a shimmering *mezza voce* with the effect of tender intimacy.

Strauss: TOMORROW (Morgen), p. 111

Style—sustained legato

Tone color—dark and warm

Mood—tender contemplative reverie

While this noble composition is considered outstanding even in the company of the world's greatest short songs, it is, nevertheless, not beyond the capabilities of a first-year student for effective rendition, especially if the optional phrasing indicated is employed and a sensitive accompanist is available. Rich warm tone, sustained legato, accurate rhythm and intonation, artistic feeling, and fine balance with the accompaniment are required. Note that the long, lovely introduction is repeated exactly to form a haunting accompaniment for the vocal line.

Strauss: TO YOU (Zueignung), p. 117

Style—lyric sostenuto

Tone color—dark and warm

Mood—tender veneration and love, exaltation

This tender love song with the wonderful rhapsodic ending is justly well beloved as a concert favorite. The second verse should be somewhat louder and faster in tempo than the first, while the third verse should start slower and end faster in the last three measures. Sing the last ''Thanks, dear heart,'' full voice with exaltation. Lotte Lehmann recommended that the last tone be held and released simultaneously with the final piano chord. The prevailing tone color is dark. However, the second verse should be brighter and the final phrase ringingly brilliant. Piano accompaniment is not difficult except for the fourth, fifth, and sixth measures from the end. Unless the accompanist is an extremely ready sight reader he or she should practice and memorize this very tough section. The interlude between the second and last verses offers the pianist opportunity for a short but very eloquent solo passage.

Wolf: SECRECY (Verborgenheit), p. 124

Style—sustained legato

Tone color—dark but intense, not gloomy

Mood—contemplative sadness

While marked ''slowly'' in tempo, this song had best be taken by the majority of singers only slightly slower than *moderato* for the most effective rendition. In the ''A'' section, the mood is quiet and contemplative with long flowing phrases that demand the maximum of sustained *legato* technic. The contrasting ''C'' section starts quietly and builds up to a magnificent climax before the recapitulation of the ''A'' section, perfecting the formal structure. It is suggested that the recapitulation be even softer than the original statement for the most effective interpretation.

Modern French Impressionistic

Debussy: EVENING FAIR (Beau Soir), p. 127

> Style—sustained lyric
>
> Tone color—dark and suave
>
> Mood—contemplative and peaceful

Debussy originated a new and evolutionary mode of style and musical expression called "Impressionism," which not only exerted a profound influence on later modern French composers but also on the entire world of musical composition. Although the music is not dramatic in the usual sense of the word, it moves the listener deeply with a strangely fascinating spell. The delicate expression is characterized by subtle suggestiveness, mystical dreams, fleeting moods, intangible sensuousness, the shimmer of moonlight on water, the pale glow of the moon, fog, silence, and so forth. "Beau Soir" is typical of Debussy's style of expression and is his most popular concert song. It should be taken at a leisurely tempo, but not too slowly. Only the one phrase at the *animando poco a poco crescendo* is quite taxing on breath control if it is ended *forte* as intended. The tone color on the last phrase, "While we to the tomb," should be very dark, even sepulchral in quality.

Fauré: AFTER A DREAM (Après un rêve), p. 130

> Style—sustained lyric legato
>
> Tone color—dark, warm and suave
>
> Mood—veiled mystery, contemplative love

This is not only a first-class song for the concert repertoire, but also an excellent study to develop suave *pianissimo* tone and the ability to sustain long, flowing phrases. While some optional breath marks are given in the editing, they are more detrimental than usual and should be avoided if possible. It is preferable to take the *andantino* tempo a little faster than to break the beauty of the long, flowing phrases. Begin with delicate ecstasy, taking care that dynamics are never overdrawn and that the mood of veiled mystery is maintained. There is only one real *forte*—on the first "Alas." Here occurs the only painful outcry and earthly reality in the song, and the tone color, which has been dark and mysterious, becomes bright and intense. Return immediately to the dark, veiled quality for the second "Alas" and for the remainder of the song.

Fauré: THE CRADLES (Les Berceaux), p. 134

> Style—sustained legato
>
> Tone color—rich mezzo, intense, sad
>
> Mood—poignant sorrow, nostalgic longing

This fine lullaby expresses both the sorrow of mothers at the departure of their seagoing husbands and the longing of the sailors to return to the "cradles" of home. The accompaniment, through a swaying movement, constantly imitates the rocking of cradles and should be played very smoothly and *legato* throughout. The text has an unusually powerful influence upon the melody with the melodic sweep of the phrase line reminiscent of the surges of the tide upon the ocean beaches. In interpretation, these surges of the melodic line must be controlled carefully so that they build up gradually, insistently, and powerfully to a soul-stirring climax. Although the song is sustained *legato* in style, do not neglect a slight accent on the first and third beats of the measure (counting four and not twelve beats to the measure). A rich, intense, *mezzo* tone should become more brightly poignant at the *piu mosso*, returning to the original *mezzo* at the *tempo primo*. The *diminuendo* at the end should literally die away in silence. The exceptionally sensitive and beautiful English translation is, in my opinion, fully as effective as the original French.

Godard: FLORIAN'S SONG (Chanson de Florian), p. 138

> Style—narrative legato
>
> Tone color—bright
>
> Mood—happy and vivacious

The tempo of this favorite concert song should be moderately quick with flowing flexible rhythm. Take care in accenting the right words and syllables and in flexible phrasing. The phrasing and dynamics for each verse are marked carefully so that suitable contrast and a fine climax may be obtained. The *portamento* carry-over between the end of the last verse and the beginning of the chorus is most effective and is a challenging exercise to develop breath support. The mood should be happy and vivacious with a sudden richening of tone and a more serious mood at the *sostenuto* on the last two phrases.

Hahn: THE EXQUISITE HOUR (L'Heure exquise), p. 142

Style—sustained lyric legato

Tone color—rich and suave

Mood—quiet, tender reflection

This is indeed an exquisite, enchanting song with a subtle, gently rocking motion in the accompaniment. Not even a *mezzo forte* is called for in the score. Beware of ruining the necessary delicacy of expression through either loud singing or sentimentality. Sing very quietly, tenderly, and intimately with the ending fading away like a gentle sigh. Caress each word as if painting a landscape with loving words. Take the second section somewhat faster than the first, and the *tranquillo* section slower.

Hahn: WERE MY SONGS WITH WINGS PROVIDED (Si mes vers avaient des ailes), p. 145

Style—lyric legato, sostenuto ending

Tone color—suavely intense

Mood—gentle introspective affection

An eloquent text by Victor Hugo is matched by an eloquent and exquisite musical setting. This delicate lyric song with the fluid *arpeggio* accompaniment is undoubtedly one of the most popular modern French songs, both in concert and for teaching purposes. The dynamics have been adjusted slightly from traditional editing in order to provide more suitable contrasts. This is an excellent song to develop *pianissimo* in the upper register; the one phrase in the third verse, in particular, "As to her nest flies a dove," is unsurpassed as practice for the difficult ascending *diminuendo* ending *pianissimo*. Practice this passage first on a favorable vowel. A warm, suave, freely produced lyric tone, and finesse in phrasing are required.

Hüe: I WEPT, BELOVED, AS I DREAMED (J'ai pleuré un rêve), p. 148

Style—sustained legato

Tone color—poignantly bright

Mood—intense grief

This song has much in common with Schumann's "I Dreamed That I Was Weeping," but reaches a much more powerful and intense climax. Begin quietly, gradually increase both dynamics and emotional intensity to the overpowering final phrase whose cry of anguish should grip the emotions of the listener as powerfully as a sob of uncontrolled grief. This is an unexcelled study song to develop dramatic emotional intensity and is an audience favorite. Students must beware that their voices are still under control and that they are not "yelling" on the *fortissimo* climax.

Lalo: THE CAPTIVE (L'Esclave), p. 151

Style—sustained lyric legato

Tone color—suave but not sombre

Mood—contemplative sadness

Only in the Modern French Impressionistic School of Song can we find a comparable rival to this type of contemplative, soft, lyric song, and none there surpass the lovely *sostenuto* ending. The tone should be *mezzo* with an intense, suave quality and should become no louder on the fortes than retention of this timbre will allow. Sing the last phrase, "As flowers fall," very slowly with maximum *sostenuto*, rich intensity of tone, and a long *fermata* and *diminuendo* that disappears like a gentle sigh. This last phrase is unsurpassed for practice of soft *sostenuto* technic.

Massenet: ELEGY (Élégie), p. 154

Style—lyric legato with dramatic climax

Tone color—bright with suave quality and frequent dark contrast

Mood—dejection

In French song literature, Massenet's "Élégie" ranks high in the favor of both audiences and students. To sing it effectively, it is necessary to give careful attention to accuracy of the syncopated rhythm in the accompaniment and the sudden and extreme changes of both dynamics and tone color. It demands more dramatic force than most French songs, but the voice should not be forced to achieve the effect. The last phrase with the sustained *crescendo-diminuendo* effect is excellent for practicing this technic.

Oratorio and Sacred

Bach: ABIDE WITH ME (Bist du bei mir), p. 157

> Style—sostenuto
>
> Tone color—rich, warm
>
> Mood—gentle worship, abiding faith, contentment

Several experienced teachers and reviewers strongly recommended that this great Bach song be added to the Sacred and Oratorio section of the new edition. With a range of an octave and a fifth and some demanding phrases at the *poco lento* tempo, it is a song of moderate difficulty. Retain the noble, gentle worshipful character of the song throughout. It is a peaceful song with it loudest dynamics marked **Mf:** it should never be dramatic or bombastic at any climax. It is appropriate for both sacred and secular occasions and appears to be equally effective in either the original German or the English translation provided. I recommend the latter when sung for most English-speaking audiences. Sing simply, forthrightly, with a warm, rich tone, and strive for steady equality of resonance in the phrase line, especially when the numerous wide-interval leaps in the melody are encountered.

Gounod: O DIVINE REDEEMER (Repentir), p. 160

> Style—dramatic, lyric in chorus
>
> Tone color—generally bright
>
> Mood—pleading, sacred veneration

Very few major composers wrote sacred songs except as incidental arias in longer sacred works. Gounod composed a number of sacred songs among which "O Divine Redeemer" is the best known and liked. It demands both dramatic and lyric technic for most effective performance and is an excellent study song for developing range and technic. The refrain section should be sung softly with pure bel canto lyricism while other parts require at times almost dramatic operatic delivery. Diction should be especially forceful in dramatic passages. The last phrase, "Help me, my Savior," should express both urgent pleading and veneration of the divine.

Handel: O LOVELY PEACE, p. 171

> Style—lyric legato with some florid passages
>
> Tone color—approaching dark, intense but not gloomy
>
> Mood—quiet dignity, tender veneration

This lovely, quiet composition from *Judas Maccabaeus* was written originally as a duet, but is a fine concert or sacred solo for medium or high voice if the melody line indicated in the editing is followed. The tone should be warm, pure, and flowing; no robust *forte* or dramatic singing is appropriate at any time. The last *adagio* passage is an excellent study exercise in slow florid style.

Handel: O SLEEP, WHY DOST THOU LEAVE ME, p. 178

> Style—lyric sostenuto
>
> Tone color—dark, intense but not gloomy
>
> Mood—quiet sadness

This aria from *Semele* is one of the loveliest arias written by the great master and is a favorite concert number sung by all voices, although written originally for baritone. Typical of Handel's style, some of the phrases are quite long. However, the aria may be sung effectively by those with inadequate breath control by electing the *ossia* phrasing indicated. A quiet, dignified, straightforward, *sostenuto* style with pure rich tone is indicated. Avoid especially any tendency to tonal stridency on the *forte* and *medium forte* climaxes on the last page.

Handel: WEEP NO MORE, p. 186

> Style—sustained legato
>
> Tonal color—dark and warm but not gloomy
>
> Mood—quiet introspection

The aria "Weep No More" from *Hercules* was written originally for mezzo-soprano, but it is good study material for any voice and a fine concert number for the singer capable of a smooth *legato* and rich tonal texture. Sing it with an intense warm tone and quiet fervor, but keep within the dramatic restraints that oratorio style imposes.

Stradella: O LORD, HAVE MERCY (Pietà, Signore), p. 181

Style—sustained legato

Tone color—bright with variations

Mood—pleading supplication

Very little is known about Stradella except that he received early recognition as a distinguished composer, lived most of his life in Venice, and after fleeing Venice with the mistress of a Venetian nobleman, was murdered by hired assassins in Genoa. Besides writing numerous songs, Stradella was also the composer of six oratorios and eleven dramatic works. His flair for the dramatic is reflected in this song, which ranks with the finest of the Old Italian School in the dramatic and eloquent setting of the text. It should be sung with deep feeling, close attention to word meaning, and (with occasional exceptions) in a rather bright tone. The ending phrase, "Eternal death," should be dark or even sepulchral in quality.

Opera

Handel—AH, POOR HEART! (Ah!, mio cor), p. 200

Style—sustained legato with some accented and dramatic passages

Tone color—bright but not shrill, some variation to dark

Mood—anguished complaint

Handel spent almost four years in Italy where he composed a number of Italian operas and became so adept in the Old Italian style that collections of Old Italian songs frequently contain some written by Handel. "Ah! mio cor" from *Alcina* is both an excellent concert and study song. The latter part of "Ah! mio cor" introduces the student to dramatic operatic idiom. However, it must be understood that this is Early Italian operatic idiom and therefore more restrained than the later Romantic School. In singing, give careful attention to delivery of the text with dramatic significance. Dynamic and other expression marks in the score plus careful analysis of word meaning should be sufficient guides to a good interpretation of this straightforward aria.

Handel: LEAVE ME TO LANGUISH (Lascia ch'io pianga), p. 190

Style—sustained legato and recitative

Tone color—warm and rich

Mood—intense sorrow

This aria from *Rinaldo* is one of Handel's most popular concert arias, and it is widely used for teaching purposes both to introduce recitative style and to develop sustained *legato*. It is usually sung in the original Italian although the English translation is excellent and often heard. While the accompaniment for the recitative introduction is sparse enough to allow free recitative and much liberty with rhythm, it should be, in this case, sung quite strictly. However, declamatory style with much attention to important word emphasis must be employed. The aria is straightforward sustained *legato* and should present no difficult problems in expression.

Monteverdi: O DEATH NOW COME (Lasciatemi morire), p. 194

Style—dramatic sostenuto

Tone color—dark with variations

Mood—anguished despair

Usually listed in Old Italian song collections, "Lasciatemi morire" is not typical of this song style since it is operatic, far too dramatic, and requires a dark sonorous tone much of the time for effective rendition. This short aria from *Arianna* is a concert favorite and used often in teaching as an excellent and easy introduction to some of the basic requirements of dramatic operatic singing. The climax phrase, "Death now come," ending the first time *forte* and the second time *fortissimo* in the score, should be sung with brilliant intensity while most of the remainder of the song employs a dark tone quality. The final phrase, "to save me," should be sung very slowly with extreme *sostenuto* and an intense, rich *mezzo* quality. Do not start this phrase so softly that it cannot be *decrescendoed* and be in no hurry to make the attack.

Purcell: DIDO'S LAMENT, p. 196

Style—recitative beginning, sustained legato in the aria

Tone color—sombre

Mood—deep sorrow and contrition

In singing this aria from *Dido and Aeneas,* remember that it is a song of death. Keep in mind the significance of each line of the text and the voice can scarcely fail to assume its proper color and intensity. The opening recitative is in free recitative style, and although the exact rhythms of Purcell's melody are difficult to improve, greater freedom at the rests is effective in indicating exhaustion and approaching death. Most of the opening recitative should be very sombre in tone color, especially "Death invades me; Death is now a welcome guest." The aria should be sung slowly, very sustained and, in the main, with sombre vocal timbre. An exception is the reiterated short phrase, "Remember me," which should be bright with a pleading intensity.

Appendix 2   Suggestions for Pronunciation

*Hints on Italian Pronunciation

Vowels

Every vowel must be pronounced distinctly in Italian; none can be omitted or slighted when two or more vowel sounds are included under one note, as is often the case. There are no diphthongs in Italian. When two or more vowels occur together, stress is placed on the principal one, the others being rapidly but distinctly sounded. Vowel stress is often indicated in modern editing. In such frequently encountered combinations as *ai, eu, oi,* and *iei,* every vowel must be pronounced distinctly. Generally speaking, Italian vowels are pronounced by the better educated natives with a very free open tone. When the Italian sings or recites poetry, he or she seems to taste and enjoy every vowel, while quickly and distinctly articulating the consonants in order that the vowel may be savored longer.

A vowel is generally **open** (long) when the syllable is **closed,** that is, it ends in a consonant, for example, *for-za, per-fet-te.* A vowel is **closed** (short) when the syllable is **open,** that is, it ends in a vowel, for example, *do-lo-re, o-no-re.* When singing, use the first pronunciation of the vowels listed below until authoritative information can be secured. A good standard dictionary in the language provides the exact meaning of the words being sung—a necessity for really convincing diction. Students wishing to sing well in a foreign language are urged first, to obtain a good English translation of the song; second, to look up the pronunciation and meaning of the words; and third, to read the foreign language over dramatically several times as a necessary preliminary key to effective interpretation, just as they should if singing the song in English.

a   like the English *ah* in *father,* never like *a* in *name* or *ball* (e.g., *ama* = ah-mah, *amor* = ah-mor).

e   usually like *e* in the English word *they,* or like *ay* in *day* without the vanishing *ee* (e.g., *pera* = pay-rah, *cena* = chay-nah).
sometimes short as *e* in *pen* (e.g., *mensa* = men-sah, *pessimo* = pes-see-moh).

i   usually like the English *ee* in *bee* (e.g., *iddio* = ee-dee-oh, *fine* = fee-nay)
sometimes short like *i* in *him* (e.g., *finire* = fin-ni-ray, *stringendo* = strin-gen-doh).

o   usually like the English exclamation *oh* without the vanishing *oo* (e.g., *corte* = koh-rtay, *popolo* = poh-poh-loh).
sometimes like *o* in *off* (e.g., *collo* = kaw-loh, *sotto* = saw-toh).

u   like *oo* in *moon* (e.g., *futuro* = foo-too-roh). When *u* precedes *o,* the sound becomes, *w* (e.g., *uomo* = wɔmo).

Consonants

Hard consonants are in general pronounced more softly than in English; soft consonants with great delicacy. The rolled *r* is difficult for English-speaking pupils as they confuse it with a gutteral sound, whereas the Italian articulates it with a quick flip of the tongue as the tongue is brought in juxtaposition with the upper teeth. A good word to use in developing this skill is *tredice* (tray-deece).

b, d, f, l, n, p, q   are pronounced as in English.

c   before *a, o,* and *u,* and before consonants it has the sound of *k* (e.g., *carro, corso, culto, creta*); before *e, i,* and *y* it has the sound of *ch* in the word *church* (e.g., *cera, citta*).

cc   before *e, i* or *y* like *ch* (e.g., *eccellenza, cerdiccio*).

ch   before *e* or *i,* like *k* (e.g., *occhio, chiesa*).

g   before *a, o,* or *u* and before consonants, like *g* in *God* (e.g., *gallo, gola, grande*); before *e* or *i* like *j* or soft as in *gem* (e.g., *genero, giro*).

gg   before *e* and *i* like *ddsh* (e.g., *corraggio, reggente*).

h   is invariably silent.

j   when used as a vowel, like Italian *i;* as a consonant, like *y* in *young.*

r   as in English, at the end of words or syllables or in combination with another consonant, but shriller and more rolling.

*These hints are offered as an aid to beginners and are generalizations covering most problems; they are not to be interpreted as an exhaustive set of rules.

sce, sco, scu   like *skay*, *ski*, *skoo* (e.g., *scala, scoria, scudo*).

sce, sci   like *shay* and *she* (e.g., *scelta, scimmia*).

z   soft, like *ds* as in *zelo, manzo*.
    sharp, like *ts* as in *zio, forza*.

Supplementary Examples of Consonant Pronunciation

c	before *a*	like *kah*	e.g., *cane* = kah-ne
	before *o*	like *ko*	e.g., *coda* = ko-da
	before *u*	like *koo*	e.g., *cuculo* = koo-koo-lo
	before *e*	like *chay*	e.g., *cece* = chay-chay
	before *i*	like *chee*	e.g., *bacino* = ba-chee-no
cc	before *e*	like *ttsche*	e.g., *accento* = a-ttshen-to
	before *i*	like *ttshee*	e.g., *occidente* = o-ttshee-den-te
ch	before *e*	like *kay*	e.g., *amiche* = ah-mee-kay
	before *i*	like *kee*	e.g., *occhio* = ok-kj-o
ci	before *a*	like *chah*	e.g., *baciamento* = bah-chu-ah-main-to
	before *o*	like *cho*	e.g., *cacio* = cah-cho
	before *u*	like *chew*	e.g., *ciurmare* = chewr-mah-ray
gh	before *e*	like *ghey*	e.g., *gorghetto* = gor-ghey-to
	before *i*	like *ghee*	e.g., *ghiro* = ghee-ro
gi	before *a*	like *jah*	e.g., *giardino* = jahr-dee-no
	before *o*	like *jo*	e.g., *giocoso* = jo-co-tso†
	before *u*	like *joo*	e.g., *giubbilo* = joob-bee-lo
gl	before *ia*	like *l'yah*	e.g., *battaglia* = baht-tah-l'yah
	before *ie*	like *l'yey*	e.g., *biglietto* = beel-l'yey-to
	before *io*	like *l'yo*	e.g., *foglio* = fol-l'yo
	before *iu*	like *l'yoo*	e.g., *pagliuca* = pah-l'yoo-kah
gn	before *a*	like *n'yah*	e.g., *vigna* = veen-yah
	before *o*	like *n'yo*	e.g., *legno* = len-yo
	before *u*	like *n'yoo*	e.g., *ignudo* = een-yoo-do
	before *e*	like *n'yay*	e.g., *igneo* = een-yay-o
	before *i*	like *n'yee*	e.g., *ogni* = ohn-yee
sch	before *e*	like *skay*	e.g., *schema* = skay-mah
	before *i*	like *skee*	e.g., *maschio* = mah-skee-o
sci	before *a*	like *shah*	e.g., *sciarpa* = shar-pah
	before *o*	like *sho*	e.g., *sciolto* = shol-to
	before *u*	like *shoo*	e.g., *sciupare* = shoo-pah-ray

(†Note: The single intervocalic *s* is voiced in singing though it may not always be so in spoken Italian.)

*Hints on German Pronunciation

German articulation and enunciation are much more forceful than that of informal English, having a more accented gutteral quality. The consonants, in particular, must be far more energetic than in English. The principal accent generally falls on the first syllable or, after prefixes, on the syllable following the prefix.

A good standard dictionary in the language provides the exact meaning of the words being sung, a necessity for really convincing diction. Students wishing to sing well in a foreign tongue are urged first, to obtain a good English translation of the song; second, to look up the pronunciation and meaning of the words; and third, to read the foreign language over dramatically several times as a necessary preliminary key to effective interpretation, just as they should if singing the song in English.

Vowels and Diphthongs

The umlaut *o* and *u* in German have no counterpart in English but are paralleled by the *eu* and the *u* in French. For the German *o* and the French *eu* the lips are rounded into the *oh* position, the base of the tongue raised into the *ay* position, and a vowel sound between the English *oh* and *ay* is sounded. For the German *u* and the French *u*, the lips are rounded into the *oo* position, the base of the tongue raised into the *ee* position, and a vowel sound between *oo* and *ee* is sounded. The German *u* leans more toward the *oo* while the French *u* is nearer *ee*.

*These hints are offered as an aid to beginners and are generalizations covering most problems; they are not to be interpreted as an exhaustive set of rules.

a   always like *ah* in *father* (e.g., *Abend* = ah-bunt, *aber* = ah-bur).

a   like *ay* before *h* and any single consonant (e.g., *ahnlich* = ayn-likh, *Hafen* = hay-fun); otherwise like *e* in *bed* (e.g., *Kamme* = kehm-muh, *andern* = ehn-durn).

ae   pronounced the same as *a* (e.g., *Aether* = ay-tur, *Aeste* = ehs-tuh).

ai   like *i* in *sigh* (e.g., *haide* = high-duh, *Mai* = my).

au   like *ow* in *how* (e.g., *Hauch* = howkh, *Auge* = ow-guh).

e   like *uh* when final and in unstressed initial syllables (e.g., *Liebe* = lee-buh, *getan* = guh-tahn).
     like *u* in inflectional endings except *e* and in unstressed noninitial syllables (e.g., *Nebel* = nay-bul, *wegen* = vay-gun).
     like *e* in *set*—(except those mentioned first above)—for prefixes (e.g., *erlauben* = ehr-low-bun, *ergaben* = ehr-gay-bun).
     like *ay* in accented syllables, before *h*, before a single consonant, and when doubled (e.g., *eher* = ay-ur, *jeder* = yay-dur, *Meer* = mayr).
     like *eh* when followed by two consonants (e.g., *Eltern* = ehl-turn, *vergessen* = fehr-gehs-sun).

ei   like *i* in *sigh* (e.g., *ein* = eign, *einsam* = ein-zahm).

eu   like *oy* in *boy* (e.g., *feurig* = foy-rikh, *euch* = oykh).

i   like *i* in *sit* as a rule (e.g., *Himmel* = him-mul, *immer* = im-mur).
     like *ee* before *h* and in *dir, Lid, mir, wir* and *wider* (e.g., *ihm* = eem, *dir* = deer).

ie   like *ee* usually (e.g., *Knie* = knee, *lieber* = lee-bur).
     sometimes like *i* in *sit* (e.g., *vierzig* = fir-tsikh, *viertel* = fir-tell).

o   like *oh* when before a single consonant, before *h*, and when final or doubled (e.g., *Forelle* = foh-rel-luh, *rot* = roht).
     otherwise like *aw* (e.g., *Dorf* = dawrf, *Gott* = gawt).

o   like *ay* with modification of *oh* position (Note: See introductory paragraph) before *h* and before a single consonant (e.g., *bose* = bay-zuh, *ode* = ay-duh, *Hohe* = hay-uh).
     like *e* in *set* elsewhere (e.g., *offnet* = ehf-nut, *Glocklein* = glehk-lighn).

oe   like *o*.

u   like *oo* before a single consonant and before *h* (e.g., *Hut* = hoot, *Blume* = bloo-muh).
     otherwise like *u* in *butter* (e.g., *Mutter* = mut-tur, *Mund* = munt).

u   like *ee* with modification of *oo* position (Note: See introductory paragraph) before *h* and before a single consonant (e.g., *vergluhen* = fehr-glee-un, *truber* = tree-bur).
     elsewhere short like *i* in a round lip position (e.g., *mussen* = mis-sun, *Furstin* = fir-stin).

ue   like *u*.

Consonants

f, h, k, l, m, p and *t*   like English.

b   like English when beginning a word or syllable.
     like *p* when the last letter of a word before a voiceless consonant such as *f* or *k*, and in the prefix *ab* (e.g., *stab* = stahp, *abgehen* = ahp-gay-un).

c   like *ts* before *a, e, i, o,* and *y* (e.g., *Cent* = tsehnt).
     like *k* elsewhere (e.g., *Cour* = koor).

ch   There is no comparable sound in English for the "front" *ch* and the "back" *ch*. In the front *ch* in such words as *dich* and *ich*, the tongue is arched upward with the tip resting easily against the lower front teeth, while the *ch* is produced with a sound somewhat like a hiss; in the back *ch* in such words as *lachen, machen*, the tongue is arched highly at the back toward the soft palate and as the tongue and palate come into close proximity, air is hissed through the opening.
     like *k* before an *s* (e.g., *fuchs* = fooks), and in words of Greek origin before *a, o, l,* or *r* (e.g., *Christ* = krist).
     like *kh* (e.g., *Milch* = milkh, *Loch* = lawkh).

ck   like *kk* (e.g., *schrecken* = shrehk-kun).

d   like English when beginning a word or syllable.
     like *t* when the last letter of a word, and before a voiceless consonant (e.g., *Lied* = leet, *Madchen* = mayt-khun).

g	like English at the beginning of a syllable or word. like *kh* in the ending *ig* (e.g., *Konig* = kay-nikh). like *k* when final and before a consonant (e.g., *klug* = klook, *Magd* = mahkt).
h	like *h* in English, but silent when final.
j	like *y* (e.g., *ja* = yah, *jeder* = yay-dur).
n	like *n* in English as a rule. like *ng* before *k* (e.g., *schenken* = shehng-kun).
q	like *kv* (e.g., *Quell* = kvell).
r	always like the trilled *r* in English
s	like English *s* when doubled, between a voiceless consonant and a following vowel, and when final (e.g., *besser* = behs-sur, *Achsel* = ahk-sul, *als* = ahls). like *z* before a vowel at the beginning of a word, between vowels, and between a voiced consonant and a following vowel (e.g., *sanft* = zahnft, *Nase* = na-zuh, *emsig* = ehm-zikh). like *sh* before *p* and *t* at the beginning of a word (e.g., *Spiele* = shpee-luh, *stand* = shtahnt).
sch	like *sh* (e.g., *schlug* = shlook, *Scheiden* = shi-dun).
th	like *t* (e.g., *thun* = toon.)
v	normally like *f* (e.g., *Vater* = fah-tur, *viel* = feel). like *v* in words of foreign origin (e.g., *Klavier* = klah-veer).
w	like *v* (e.g., *was* = vahs, *Walt* = vahlt).
x	like *ks* (e.g., *Hexe* = Hehk-suh).
y	like *ee* (e.g., *Cypresse* = tsee-prehs-suh).
z	like *ts* (e.g., *zu* = tsoo, *zart* = tsahrt).

*Hints on French Pronunciation

French is a much more nasal language than Italian, German, or English and is excellent for helping to correct voices that have a tendency to be too breathy or gutteral in production. The nasal vowels have no English equivalents. They are enunciated by saying the vowel and at the same time allowing some breath to escape through the nose and not by the inclusion of the *m, n,* or *ng* as is sometimes erroneously assumed. French vowels should usually be nasalized as described if there is a single *m* or *n* in the same syllable following the vowel; but if *m* or *n* precedes the vowel, or is doubled, or if *mn* occurs, there is usually no nasality in production.

Sounds of the French language should be formed with greater precision, vigor, clarity and suavity than is common in informal English. Vowels should be uniform throughout their utterance without any diphthongization characteristic of English. Therefore, the student should be careful not to change tongue or lip position once the vowel is formed. French differs also from English, Italian, and German in that all syllables normally have uniform or nearly equal stress. While the final *e* is silent in French speech, it is often used by composers in songs as a final syllable, in which case it is given the sound of *uh*.

A good standard dictionary in the language provides the exact meaning of words being sung, a necessity for really convincing diction. Students wishing to sing well in a foreign tongue are urged first, to obtain a good English translation of the song; second, to look up the pronunciation and meaning of the words; and third, to read the foreign language over several times dramatically as a necessary preliminary key to effective interpretation, just as they should if singing the song in English.

Vowels

a and *à*	like *a* in *path* or somewhat broader (e.g., *ami* = a-mee, *canard* = ka-nar). like *ah* when preceding a final *s* (e.g., *bas* = bah, *cas* = kah). like *ah* nasalized (Note: See introductory paragraph) when followed by *m, n,* or *ng* (e.g., *ambre* = ahbr, *errant* = eh-rah).
â	usually like *ah* (e.g., *château* = shah-toh, *relâche* = ruh-lahsh).
ai and *aï*	like *e* in *met* (e.g., *esprit* = ehs-pree, *airain* = eh-reh).
au	like *oh* usually (e.g., *aussi* = oh-see, *berceau* = behr-soh).
e	(mute) like *uh* (e.g., *petit* = puh-teet, *cerise* = suh-reez), or silent when final (e.g., *plaine* = plehn, *cerise* = suh-reez).

*These hints are offered as an aid to beginners and are generalizations covering most problems; they are not to be interpreted as an exhaustive set of rules.

é and ê (acute and circumflex)   like *a* in *day* (e.g., *école* = ay-kohl, *équipée* = ay-kip-ay).

è   (grave) like *e* in *set* (e.g., *excès* = ek-seh, *guère* = gehr).

ê   (circumflex) like *e* in *set* (e.g., *fête* = feht, *rêver* = reh-vay).

i   nearly always as *ee* (e.g., *livre* = lee-vr, *vie* = vee).
    usually like *y* when preceding another vowel (e.g., *grenier* = gruh-nyay).
    like *eh* when nasalized (Note: See introductory paragraph, p. 221) by a following *m* or *n* (e.g.,
    festin = fehs-teh, *important* = eh-pawr-tah).

o   usually like *aw* (e.g., *coloré* = kay-law-ray, *montrer* = maw-tray).
    like *oh* when the last sound of a word (e.g., *Pierrot* = pyeh-roh, *chose* = shohz), and before *s* (e.g.,
    oser = oh-zay, *rosier* = roh-zyay).

ô   (circumflex) like *oh* (e.g., *môtif* = moh-teef, *nôtre* = nohtr).

oeu   like *ay* in the *oh* position (e.g., *boeux* = bay, *voeu* = vay).
    like *eh* in the *aw* position (e.g., *oeuf* = ehf).

oi   usually like *wa* (e.g., *courtois* = koor-twa, *choir* = shwar).
    like *weh* when nasalized (Note: See introductory paragraph) by a following *n* (e.g., *foin* = fweh, *loin* = lweh).

ou   usually like *oo* (e.g., *bouquet* = boo-key, *nouveau* = noo-voy).
    like *w* when before another vowel (e.g., *grenouille* = gruh-nweey, *oui* = wee).

u   usually like *ee* nasalized in the *oo* position (e.g., *rue* = ree, *superbe* = see-pehrb). Note: See discussion of the
    French *u* and German *u* on p. 219.
    like *y* when followed by another vowel (e.g., *muable* = my-abl, *nuages* = nyazh, *nuit* = nyi.
    like [œ] when made nasal by a following *m* or *n* (e.g., *humble* = uhbl, *chacun* = sha-kuh).

Consonants

b   usually like *b* in English.
    like *p* before *c, s,* and *t* (e.g., *absent* = ap-sah, *obtenir* = awp-tuh-neer).

c   usually like *k* (e.g., *cache* = kash, *coeur* = kehr).
    like *s* before *e, i,* and *y* (e.g., *celle* = sehl, *ciel* = syehl), and when cedilla is indicated (e.g.,
    garcon = gahr-saw).

cc   pronounce the first *c* hard and the other soft when followed by *e, i,* or *y* (e.g., *accident* = ak-see-dah,
    succès = syk-say).

d   usually like *d* in English, but the French *d* is more dental.
    like *t* when linked (e.g., *prendil* = prah-teel).

f   like *f* in English.

g   nearly always as *g* (e.g., *glisser* = glee-say).
    like *zh* before *e, i,* and *y* (e.g., *gage* = gazh, *agir* = a-zheer).

gg   pronounce the first *g* hard and the other soft when followed by *e, i,* or *y* (e.g., *suggérer* = syg-jay-ray).

gn   usually like *ny* (e.g., *règne* = reh-ny).

h   usually silent.
    sometimes aspirate *h* in words of Teutonic origin (e.g., *haler* = hah-lay).

j   like *zh* (e.g., *je* = zhuh, *jambe* = zhahb).

k   like *k* in English.

l   usually like *l* in English, but more dental.

m   usually like *m* in English except when silent *if preceding another consonant (e.g., *trompette* = traw-peht).

n   usually like *m* in English except it is silent *when final or before another consonant (e.g., *maman* = mah-mah,
    confier = kaw-fyay).

p   like *p* in English.

ph   like *f* in English (e.g., *philosophe* = fee-law-zawf, *phare* = far).

*However, it causes the preceding vowel to be nasal.

q and **qu**   like *k* (e.g., *cinq* = sehk, *quel* = kehl).

r   like *r* in English.

s   usually like *s* in English (e.g., *Sabbath* = sah-bah, *savoir* = sa-vwar).
like *z* between vowels (e.g., *désir* = day-zeer, *desert* = day-zehr).
like *z* when linked (e.g., *ignobles entraves* = ee-nyaw-bluhzah-trav).

ss   always like *s* in English (double flipped).

t   usually like *t* in English (e.g., *tableux* = ta-bloh).
like *s* in terminations having *ti* followed by a vowel (e.g., *nation* = nah-seeaw, *action* = ak-seeaw. Exceptions:
adjectives and nouns ending in *tie* have the normal *t* sound (e.g., *sortie* = sawr-tee).

th   like *t* in English (e.g., *thé* = tay, *thème* = tehm).

v   like *v* in English.

w   normally not in French except in words from a foreign source where it is pronounced as *v* (e.g., *warrant* =
va-ra, *wagon* = va-gaw).

x   like *ks* before a consonant and between vowels (e.g., *exprimer* = eks-pree-may, *oxygene* = awk-see-zehn).
like *k* before *ce* and *ci* (e.g., *excellent* = ek-seh-lah).
like *gz* after *e* and preceding a vowel (e.g., *exalter* = ayg-zal-tay).

y   usually like *y* before a vowel (e.g., *payer* = peh-yay, *pays* = pay-ee.
sometimes like a vowel (e.g., *mystère* = mee-stayr, *martyr* = mahr-teer, *symbol* = seh-bawl, *thym* = teem.

z   like *z* in English.

Glossary of Music Terms[*]

Accel. *Accelerando* or *accelerato*—gradually faster.

Adagio Slow tempo between *andante* and *largo*.

Ad. Lib. *Ad libitum*—free and flexible with tempo and note value.

Affettuoso With emphasis.

Agility Ability to execute rapid passages nimbly and quickly.

Agitato Agitated.

Allargando Slowing down gradually.

Allegretto Tempo between andante and allegro.

Allegro Fast tempo.

Andante Walking speed; tempo between allegretto and adagio.

Andantino Diminutive of andante; somewhat quicker than andante.

Animando *Animato*—spirited.

Animato *Animando*—spirited.

Appassionata With passion, emotional fervor.

Assai Much, very.

A tempo Return to the tempo that prevailed just before the tempo change.

Bel canto A style of singing characterized by lyricism, legato, pure vowels, and freedom of production that originated in Italy during the so-called Golden Age of Song (from 1685–1825). It is also used mistakenly to denote a style of vocal instruction attributed to the Old Italian Masters.

Ben With

Brio Spirit and vigor.

Cantabile In a lyric, legato singing style.

Coda The ending section (usually short) after all repeats.

Colla voce Indication directing player of the accompaniment to "follow along" with the main voice part.

Con With.

Con affetto With affection.

Con moto With motion.

Cres. (or cresc.) *Crescendo*—gradually louder.

Delicatamente Delicately.

D. C. *Da capo*—return to the beginning.

Decres. *Decrescendo*—gradually softer.

Diction The overall descriptive term that includes pronunciation, enunciation, and articulation.

Dim. *Diminuendo*—gradually softer

Diphthong A compound of two vowel sounds produced as one syllable.

Dolce Sweetly, softly.

Dolciss Sweetly.

Dolente Sorrowfully.

Doloroso Sadly, sorrowfully.

Dynamics Force or degree of loudness.

Ed And.

Energico With energy in tempo and dynamics.

Espress With expression.

Espressivo Expressively.

Flexibility Ability of the vocal instrument to adjust freely to sudden changes in pitch, dynamics or timbre; it includes agility but incorporates much more.

Florid Vocal music that is ornamental, embellished, or virtuoso in style.

Giocoso Jocose, humorous, cheerful.

Glissando A "scooping" slurring method of connecting two pitches.

Grandioso In a grand manner, broadly.

Gravita Solemn.

Grazia Graceful style of performance.

Guisto With vigor.

Interpretation The total act of musical expression in communicating mood, thought, and musical values.

Intimo Intimately.

Largamente Broadly.

Larghetto Somewhat faster than largo.

Largo Very slow tempo.

Legato A style of singing basic to most songs and singing practice. Tones flow in a smooth vocal line with no apparent interference from articulation. It is characterized by a very light portamento connecting tones on different pitches.

Lento Slow.

Lunga Hold note a long time.

Marcato Markedly, emphasize.

Mezza voce Half-voice, a soft, subdued tonal effect.

[*]Terms obtained from all the songs and the "Suggestions for Interpretation" sections of the Appendixes from the song anthologies of *Expressive Singing*, Vol. I and Vol. II.

Moderato   Moderately fast tempo, faster than andante.

Molto   Much.

Mosso   Speed. (Meno mosso-less speed; più mosso-more speed)

Moto   Pace, motion.

Ossia   Or.

Parlando   Speaking, indication in singing scores that vocal production is to approximate speech in style.

Phrasing   Everything that is done interpretively to the musical phrase to make it expressive and meaningful.

Più   More.

Più meno mosso   Somewhat less speed of tempo.

Poco a poco   Somewhat, little by little.

Pomposo   Pompously, broadly.

Portamento   An artistically controlled ''glide'' between two tones that is executed consciously in its ''extreme'' and ''medium'' types of movement. In its ''light'' type glide, characteristic of good legato singing, it becomes an habitually unconscious method of melody production. It is not to be confused with the slower moving ''slur'' or ''glissando.''

Pure vowel   A correct pure vowel sound without diphthongization.

Rall.   *Rallentando*—gradually slower; same as rit—*ritardando*.

Range   Compass of the voice, extent of pitches that can be sung.

Recit.   *Recitative*—in a declamatory manner with emphasis on speech values.

Religioso   In a sincere, worshipful manner.

Rinf.   *Rinforzando*—a sudden strong accent on a single note or chord.

Rit.   *Ritardando*—gradually slower; same as rall.—*rallentando*.

Simili   Similarly.

Sin′ al   Until the. *Sin′ al fine* (until the end). *Sin′ al segno* (until the sign).

Slur   A scooping glissando effect; a slow, lazy gliding from one tone to another.

Sombre   Dark gloomy tone color.

Sostenuto   To sustain or hold tones steady and connect them in the phrase line without dynamic letdown between tones.

Staccatto   Lightly accented, disconnected style in singing or playing—the opposite to legato.

Stent.   *Stentato*—Stentorious, loudly.

String.   *Stringendo*—gradually increase tempo to the climax.

Tempo   Rate of speed of a musical composition.

Tempo primo   Return to the tempo of the beginning.

Ten.   *Tenuto*—to linger somewhat on the note but not enough to add a beat as in a fermata (hold).

Tessitura   The average or prevailing part of the compass of a melody or voice part in which most of the tones lie; range where the most characteristic part of the voice appears to lie.

Tranquillo   Tranquilly, calmly, gently.

Vivace   Vivaciously, lively, quickly.